COPYRIGHT INFORMATION

"You got to realize; you're the Devil as much as you're a God" –
Charles Manson.

ACKNOWLEDGEMENTS

The author acknowledges that when writing on such a topic matter, as is contained in this book, it can be a very touchy subject.

Memories flooding back, close run-ins with your own brush with death, or a family member or friend who may have fallen victim.

After all they say that throughout your lifetime you walk past a murderer 36 times, and so you could have easily been one of the names added to the victim list throughout the following pages.

This book is in no way an attempt to showcase or add further to the notoriety of those contained within, however is primarily written as an educational tool.

The best way to honour those who we have lost over time is re-telling their story, telling the story behind those who have caused horror across the world through various means.

If we can save just one person because we have opened their eyes, or upon reading this book they see some educational purpose on how better to protect themselves, or to seek help if they have fallen down the spiral slope to what many would call the 'Dark Side' then this book ('HORROR AND THOSE WHO CAUSED IT') has served its purpose.

The author however would like to acknowledge the support that he has received for the works contained within, as well as acknowledge the friends and family of those who fell victim to those who are not only contained within these pages but who have had their lives taken at the hands of another.

DEDICATION

First and foremost, I would like to dedicate this book to the victims. Without you we would not have these murderers sitting in a jail cell.

To the friends and family of the victims I thank you for being open when discussing with me your plight, and as many of you have stated to me I do hope that this book comes to some use in the memories of the loved ones that you have lost.

As an author, and someone who takes his profession seriously, off course I have hundreds of hours invested in this book through research, meeting and talking to the victims' families and even corresponding with some of the subjects of the focus of this book.

None of that would have been possible without the support of my fantastic fiancée, children, and my ever-growing extended family who have backed me and supported me from the very beginning.

INTRODUCTION

I sat here hesitantly, my fingers wavering over my keyboard as I exchanged glances between it and the monitor that sit on top of the computer desk.

In the background *Spotify* with my usual work playlist that assists in getting my head in the right place it needs to be to begin writing.

As a generally outgoing person who enjoys having a laugh, meet new people and have a good time it is near impossible as a Horror author for me to get into that dark mindset that is required from me to achieve the best results for my stories.

It's weird but when I write I almost go into a self-imposed trance, I have music that gets me to slip to the dark side, have the dark thoughts, and get the mind and fingers pumping...

And then come the end of each day I am required to spend almost half-an-hour to bring me out of the trance, to bring me from the dark side back to my happy, easy going, usual jovial self.

But on this day things were different, I wasn't creating stories from the dark regions and thoughts in my head – geez if what was retold throughout these pages were figments of my imagination the world would be a much better place, and I'd probably be living the high life rather than just covering the bills.

Where was I to start? What order do I write them in? What constitutes too much detail that takes it from a general informative book to a gore-fest that wouldn't be suitable for the feint-hearted.

This book is in no way aimed at adding to the notoriety of killers, serial killers or religious cult leaders – they get far too much publicity as it stands.

And, in no way am I attempting to glorify what they have done which has put them as some of the major talking points whenever anyone talks about killings, or cults.

It is imperative for you to know that I am here after twenty-something years of this interest putting my fingers to the keyboard on what I know and looking to close off this chapter in my life.

Macabre, or just completely wrong to have an interest in this subject? I don't think any of us have the answers, after all there is a reason you brought this book to read.

A serial killer is most commonly described as a person who commits a series of murders, often with no apparent motive and typically following a characteristic, predictable behaviour pattern.

While a cult is often described as a system of religious veneration and devotion directed towards a figure or object.

So, what makes learning, reading and writing about serial killers, cults and those who have caused horrific acts across the world, such a unique, thought provoking genre?

Is it simply, especially today, the desire to know the details? That with technology the way it is that we now demand to know the details with the very touch of a button?

Or is it simply trying to understand how 'normal' people seem to give their complete devotion to someone who claims to be the second coming of Christ? Or how one gets themselves to the point where killing others – and at times multiple persons –

is their way of dealing with whatever depths of torture their mind has found itself in.

We, as an ever-growing society which is facing horrific acts on an almost daily basis, need to take a moment to honour those who have perished, while at the same time working hard to understand.

Will we ever stop horrific acts being conducted across the globe? The real answer is No. But are we able to consider what has caused people to get so desperate these are the acts they have taken? Possibly.

This book is not a "Who Shot John," nor will it take your hand and very basically outline the targets of this book – if you are reading this book no doubt you have read others and can agree that those type of books have been done.

You know you have been there read them. And if you haven't we all know Google and Wikipedia are your best friend when it comes to research or for interesting articles, essays or books to read on the subjects contained within these pages.

No.

What this book is trying to achieve is to dig deeper, provide you a story to immerse yourself in to allow you to picture and can feel what those who have fallen victim have felt.

The details are taken from Police Records, transcripts, many letters sent backwards and forwards between myself and the subjects of this book and speaking to survivors and/or family members of those who have lost their lives.

THE PEOPLES TEMPLE

It had been an exhausting few days for those that called Jonestown in the North-western Guyana home, they had been preparing for the arrival of Congressman Leo Ryan, a delegation of media journalists and family members of some of the members they lived side-by-side with at the compound.

This meant preparing the grounds, and the sleeping quarters in which the 53-year-old Congressman Leo Ryan – who just eleven-days earlier had been re-elected to his fourth term in office – and others from his delegation would reside in during their visit.

The usual meals consisting of rice for breakfast, rice water soup for lunch, and rice for dinner in the preparation stage of being replaced with a more gourmet offering to satisfy their illustrious guests.

Little did they know, those long hard days working throughout the compound, would be the last time they would have to tend to the fields that many of the followers had done so since the group first rented the land in 1974.

It was November 17th, 1978 – and within twenty-fours over 900-members who had flooded the Jonestown site for a better and more meaningful life under the guidance of Reverend Jim Jones would take their lives after a rousing final sermon from their leader encouraged them to drink Kool Aid laced with Cyanide.

Most of the religious followers were dead within fifteen minutes of drinking their laced cups.

The leader of the religious group was Reverend Jim Jones, born in Crete, Indianapolis on May 13th, 1931 to James Thurman

Jones (1887 – 1951), a World War I veteran, and Lynetta Putnam (1902 – 1977).

In 1934, at the height of the Great Depression Jones' family were forced to move into a shack without any plumbing in the town of Lynn where he grew up and developed an avid interest in reading.

Joseph Stalin, Karl Marx, Mao Zedong, Mahatma Ghandi, and Adolf Hitler, were among the subjects of which he had taken an avid interest in, noting each of their strengths and weaknesses.

Finding it difficult to make friends a young Jim Jones turned his interest towards religion. Childhood friends would later recount that Jones was a *"really weird kid"* who was *"obsessed with religion... obsessed with death."*

Jones disassociated himself from his alcoholic father after he learned of his father's Ku Klux Klan involvement, with the Reverend later claiming that he didn't speak to his father for *"many, many years"*.

When his parents separated Jim Jones moved with his mother to Richmond where in December 1948 he graduated from Richmond High School early with honours.

The following year Jones married nurse Marceline Baldwin (1927 – 1978) with the couple soon moving to Bloomington, Indiana where Jones attended Indiana University Bloomington.

That was until a rousing speech by Eleanor Roosevelt about the plight of African-Americans impressed him, prompting him to move to Indianapolis in 1951 where he attended night school earning a degree in secondary education from Butler University in 1961.

In 1952 Jim Jones became a student pastor in Sommerset Southside Methodist Church, but later claimed he left the church because its leaders barred him from integrating blacks into his congregation.

It was around this time that he witnessed a faith-healing service at a Seventh Day Baptist Church. He observed that it attracted people and money and concluded that, with financial resources from such healings, he could help accomplish his own social goals.

Jones organized a mammoth religious convention to take place on June 11th – 15th 1956. To draw the crowds he needed a religious headliner and so he arranged to share the pulpit with Reverend William M. Branham (1909 – 1965), a healing evangelist and religious author.

Such was the popularity of convention Jim Jones was able to launch his own church which changed its name numerous times until it settled on the Peoples Temple Christian Church Full Gospel.

To increase the publicity of his church the Peoples Temple Christian Church Full Gospel – or as often referred to – 'The Peoples Temple' continued to organize religious conventions with other Pentecostal pastors with as many as 11 000 followers and believers attending the events.

The Temple stressed egalitarian ideals, asking members to attend in casual clothing so poor members would not feel out of place. Even going as far as providing shelter to the needy.

In February 1960 the Temple opened a soup kitchen for the poor before expanding to offer such services as rent assistance, job placement services, free canned goods, clothing and coal for winter heating. Though the efforts of Jones and his wife the soup kitchen found itself on average providing 2 800 meals a month.

The Temples underlying "us versus them" message was first relayed by Reverend Jim Jones after finding the teachings of Father Devine (1876 – 1965) – founder of the International Peace Mission Movement – of whom Jones studied his writings and recordings of his sermons.

The church quickly adopted the stance that members should abstain from sexual intercourse and should only adopt children.

Following a visit by some Temple members to Father Devine the church began printing his teachings to spread the word and leading to a sermon by Reverend Jim Jones at his Delaware Street Temple that is widely regarded to have shaped the new direction in which the church was going in.

His sermon in 1959 captivated members with lulls and crescendos, as Jones challenged individual members in front of the congregation.

It led to the Temple to begin tightening their organisation, asking more of its members than any other church. It required members to spend important holidays such as Thanksgiving and Christmas with its Temple 'family' rather than with blood relatives.

Jones then began to offer the congregation a deal towards "religious communalism" in which members would donate their material possessions to the Temple in exchange for the Temple all those member' needs.

It was also during this period and into 1960 that the Temples religious message transitioned between atheism and subtle references to its leader being a Christ-like figure.

Over the following years the Temple's membership continued to grow with the church claiming over 20 000 members, although more realistic numbers suggest in the realm of 3 000 –

5 000 members on the books at the time of the church being dissolved following the Mass Suicide at Jonestown in 1978.

By the mid 1970's the church boasted locations in Redwood Valley, Los Angeles and San Francisco.

With satellite congregations in almost a dozen other locations around the country with Jones often referring to locations such as: Ukiah – Los Angeles, Bakersfield – Fresno, and Sacramento. The Temple also maintained a branch, college tuition program, and dormitory at Santa Rosa Junior College.

During this time Jim Jones and the Peoples Temple earned recognition for aiding the cities' poorest citizens, especially racial minorities, drug addicts and the homeless.

With growing speculation around the church following some high-profile defections, including what is widely referred to as the 'Gang of Eight' of whom mainly young members defected from the church, the paranoia from the leader and others in his advisement panel began to grow.

Following a letter written by the 'Gang of Eight' of mistreatment inside the church, and double standards, authorities began to investigate the church and it was heavily rumoured that an investigation was underway to the legality of the churches tax-exemption status.

It was reported that at some stage during this period The Peoples Temple was receiving more than $65 000 in Social Security Checks, while other members who were capable of working were giving as much as 25% of their wage to the church.

Fearing the repercussions from such an investigation, and despite assurances from San Francisco Mayor George Mascone (1929 – 1979) that the city would not investigate the church, the publishing of unflattering articles in the San Francisco Examiner and Indianapolis Star – which included an expose on church dealings, its claims of healings, and Jim Jones' ritual of throwing the Bible down in church, yelling, *"This black book has held you people down for 2 000-years. It has no powers."* – led Jones and his advisory panel to step up their hunt for a more permanent location for the church to set up without the growing scrutiny they had found themselves under.

In 1974 the Peoples Temple signed a lease to rent land in Guyana.

The community established on this property and was named the *"Peoples Temple Agricultural Project"*, or unofficially, *"Jonestown"*.

After travelling to an area of North-western Guyana with Guyanese officials, Reverend Jim Jones and the Temple negotiated the lease of 3 800 acres (km²) of jungle land located 150 miles (240km) west of the Guyanese capital of Georgetown.

The site was isolated and had soil of low fertility, even by Guyanese standards. The nearest body of water was seven miles (11km) and was only accessible by travel across muddy roads.

Jonestown's location stood not far from the disputed Guyanese border with Venezuela.

With Guyanese officials secretly hopeful that the presence of American citizens would deter any Venezuelan plans of military incursion.

Later in 1974 Guyanese officials granted the Temple with permission to import certain items "duty free".

Later payoffs helped safeguard shipments of firearms and drugs through Guyanese customs.

As church leader Reverend Jim Jones then negotiated with officials to permit the mass-migration of The Peoples Temple.

To secure the permission Jones stated the members were "skilled and progressive," and offered an envelope which he claims held $500 000 in cash, also claiming that The Peoples Temple and its congregation would invest most of the groups assets into Guyana.

Soon after safe passage was granted to the Temples members, where at its peak in 1978 an estimated 1 000 members had relocated to the 'Peoples Temple Agricultural Project', members noticed a shift in the Temples teachings.

Children would wake at 6a.m. to begin work in the fields at 7, they would continue their work until early afternoon where they would be given an hour for lunch – this time was usually spent walking from the section of land that they were working to where the main buildings were.

Following lunch, they would attend school within the compound for much of the afternoon before being required to undertake Biblical Studies and Meetings where it is said that Reverend Jim Jones would talk, most of the time babbling or incoherently, for many hours.

While Jonestown was described as being "*dedicated to live for socialism, total economic and racial and social equality. We are here living communally*" by Marceline, the wife of Reverend Jim Jones, the ever-declining stability of the religious sects' leader was becoming more apparent to everyone in his day-to-day presence.

Jim Jones continuously spoke at length with his members claiming that the CIA [Central Intelligence Agency] and other intelligent agencies were conspiring with "capitalist pigs" to destroy the settlement and harm its inhabitants.

Adding to these he began testing the faithfulness of his followers.

Working them hard throughout the day, cutting most of the Jonestown occupants off from the outside, with those seen to be tired, weak and often with bags under their eyes rewarded for what he deemed to be "showing dedication" to the Temple.

The reverend further tested his pull over the members of the Temple when he began "*White Night*" drills in which he would openly claim that the CIA and the intelligent agencies were in the jungle about to encroach the camp and the members had to come to a quick decision on the course of action they were to take.

He would continue to offer four choices, being: attempt to flee to the Soviet Union, commit "revolutionary suicide", stay in Jonestown and fight the purported attackers, or take their chances of not being found and flee into the jungle.

Temple defector Deborah Layton stated in an affidavit what happened one night when the member base who had gathered voted to commit a "revolutionary suicide".

Everyone, including the children, was told to line up. As we passed through the line, we were given a small glass of red liquid to drink.

We were told that the liquid contained poison and that we would die within 45 minutes.

We all did as we were told.

When the time came when we should have dropped dead, Rev. Jones explained that the poison was not real and that we had just been through a loyalty test.

He warned us that the time was not far off when it would become necessary for us to die by our own hands.

Amid a custody battle between Tim and Grace Stoen and Reverend Jim Jones in relation to their five-year-old son John Stoen the Stoen's, alongside fellow defector Jeannie Mills launched the Concerned Relatives group.

The Concerned Relatives group throughout 1977 and 1978 engaged in letter writing campaigns to the U.S. Secretary of State and the Guyanese government.

Tim Stoen travelled to Washington D.C in a bid to begin an investigation into Jim Jones and the Peoples Temple religious commune.

In early 1978 Stoen, on behalf of the Concerned Relatives group, wrote a white paper that he presented to Congress detailing his grievances and requesting that Congressman write to Guyana Prime Minister Burnham.

As a result, 91 congressmen, including Congressman Leo Ryan wrote to the Guyanese government.

On April 11th, 1978, the Concerned Relatives group distributed a packet of documents, including letters and affidavits, that they titled "*Accusations of Human Rights Violations by Rev. James Warren Jones*" to members of the Peoples Temple, members of the press, and members of Congress.

Leo Ryan announced that he would soon visit the **Peoples Temple Agricultural Project**, he had been a friend of the father of Bob Houston, a temple member in California, whose mutilated body was found lying near train tracks on October 5th, 1976.

The discovery of the body came just three days after a taped telephone conversation between Houston and his wife in which leaving the Peoples Temple was discussed.

Over the following months Ryan's interest in what was happening at the **Peoples Temple Agricultural Project** was piqued further following the revelations and allegations made by the Stoens, Layton and the Concerned Relatives group.

On November 14th Congressman Ryan, along with eighteen others including **Jackie Speier**, then Ryan's legal adviser; Neville Annibourne, representing Guyana's Ministry of Information; Richard Dwyer, **Deputy Chief of Mission** of the U.S. embassy to Guyana; San Francisco Examiner reporter Tim Reiterman; Examiner photographer Greg Robinson; **NBC** reporter **Don Harris**; NBC camera operator Bob Brown; NBC audio technician Steve Sung; NBC producer Bob Flick; Washington Post reporter Charles Krause; San Francisco Chronicle reporter Ron Javers; and Concerned Relatives representatives, including Tim and Grace Stoen, Steve and Anthony Katsaris, Beverly Oliver, Jim Cobb, Sherwin Harris, and Carolyn Houston Boyd, flew to the nearby Port Kaituma – just seven miles from the established Jonestown.

More than 900 religious followers called Jonestown home by the time of Congressman Ryan's visit on November 14th, 1978.

Many had spent long hours in the fields preparing the compound for the visit.

While others, who some of the churches leaders had identified as showing an indication that they wanted to leave, were interrogated and coached into the right answers to give to the questions the church expected to come from the Congressman and his delegation.

Entertainers were put through their paces as they prepared for the performance they were entrusted to perform during the 'celebration' of the Congressman's visit.

Weary, exhausted and for most knowing that a satisfactory visit by Congressman Leo Ryan and his delegate could lead to a reprieve from the ongoing questions raised by the United States of America government, the people who called the Peoples Temple Agricultural Project home were prepared.

At first the delegation led by Congressman Leo Ryan were refused permission to enter Jonestown, However, by Friday 17th November 1978 they had informed Reverend Jim Jones that the Congressman and his delegation intended to visit Jonestown that afternoon regardless of his willingness.

Some hours later the Congressman Leo Ryan led delegation arrived at the airstrip at Port Kaituma, due to aircraft seating limitations only four members of the Concerned Relatives Group were able to accompany the Congressman on his visit into the settlement that had become widely known as Jonestown.

At first only Ryan and three others were accepted into Jonestown, before the rest were allowed in after dark where they attended a banquet and entertainment put on by members of The Peoples Temple congregation.

It was during this reception in the pavilion that Vernon Gosney and Monica Bagby – two congregation members – made their first attempt at being removed from The Peoples Temple.

As Gosney mistook NBC reporter Don Harris as the Congressman, passed a note that simply read:

"Dear Congressman, Vernon Gosney and Monica Bagby. Please help us get out of Jonestown."

From the delegation only Ryan, his legal advisor Jackie Speier, Richard Dwyer, and Neville Annibourne stayed at Jonestown overnight, the rest of the delegation were informed they would need to find alternative accommodation.

For the other travellers who made up the delegation, including the Press Corps and members of the Concerned Relatives Group, they travelled the seven miles back to Port Kaituma where they were offered accommodation at a small café.

In the early morning of Saturday 18th November eleven temple members could sense growing danger and walked out of the Jonestown compound.

They caught a train to the town of Matthew's Ridge, located in the opposite direction of Port Kaituma airstrip.

Those defectors included members of Jones' head of security Joe Wilson, family.

When members of the Press Corps and the Concerned Relatives Group arrived at Jonestown later that day they were given a tour of the settlement by Marceline Jones.

That afternoon the Parks and Bogue families, along with in-laws Christopher O'Neal and Harold Cordell, stepped forward and asked to be escorted out of the Jonestown by the Ryan delegation.

When Jones' adopted son Johnny attempted to talk Jerry Parks out of leaving Parks told him, *"No way, it's nothing but a communist prison camp."*

Reverend Jim Jones gave the two families, along with Gosney and Bagby, permission to leave Jonestown.

Emotional scenes developed between family members. Al Simon, a native American Temple member, attempted to take his two children to Ryan to process the requisite paperwork to transfer back to the United States of America.

Al's wife, Bonnie, summoned on the loud speaker system by Temple staff, loudly denounced her husband.

Al pleaded with Bonnie to return with him to the United States, but she rejected his suggestions.

While most of the Ryan delegation begun to depart Jonestown on the back of a large dump truck to the Port Kaituma airstrip, Ryan and Dwyer stayed behind to continue processing those who had expressed a desire to leave.

Among them was Temple loyalist Larry Layton, brother to Deborah Layton, who demanded to be on the truck as it was leaving.

Some defectors voiced their suspicion and concern about Layton's motives however, Congressman Ryan permitted him to board the truck.

As the large dump truck departed Temple member Don "Ujara" Sly grabbed Ryan while wielding a knife.

While Ryan was unhurt in the incident as other Temple members fought Sly off him, the **Deputy Chief of Mission** of the U.S. embassy to Guyana Richard Dwyer suggested that the Congressman leave Jonestown while he filed criminal charges against Don Sly.

The truck, which had departed, stopped once word reached them about the attack on Congressman Ryan and picked him up as a passenger before continuing their short journey to the airstrip.

The delegation had originally scheduled a 19-passenger Twin Otter from Guyana Airways to fly them back to Georgetown, however, with the increased numbers of defectors the United States embassy arranged for a six-passenger Cessna to help with the numbers.

When the group arrived at the airstrip between 4:30-4:45pm the two transport planes had not arrived, with the group required to wait until the planes touched down at approximately 5:10pm to begin the boarding procedures.

As the Cessna, carrying Larry Layton, Bagby, Gosney, and Dale Parks, taxied towards the far end of the airstrip for take-off Layton produced a handgun and began shooting.

He injured Bagby and Gosney and attempted to kill Dale Parks who ended up disarming him.

At approximately the same time as the rest of the delegation boarded the 19-passenger Twin Otter a tractor carrying what was widely known as the 'Red Brigade' – or the Jonestown Security detail – appeared at the airstrip.

As the tractor approached the Twin Otter, within 30 feet (9 metres), the Red Brigade opened fire upon the delegation using Shotguns, hand guns and riffles – most were firing from the tractor however, at least two Red Brigade members circled the plane on foot.

It is believed that nine Red Brigade members were involved in the attack at the airstrip – and while many of their identities remain a mystery it is widely accepted that these members included: Joe Wilson, Thomas Kice Sr. and Ronnie Davis.

The first few seconds of the shootings were captured on videotape by NBC Cameraman Bob Brown. Brown was killed along with Robinson, Harris, and Temple defector Patricia Parks in the first few minutes of the shooting.

Congressman Leo Ryan was killed after being shot a staggering twenty-times on the tarmac.

Speier, Sung, Dwyer, Reiterman, and Anthony Katsaris were all injured during the shooting however fled into nearby bushland in a desperate attempt to survive the massacre that was being played out on the airstrip.

After the shootings the pilot of the Cessna and Twin Otter fled in the Cessna to Georgetown, the damaged Otter and injured members of the Ryan delegation were left behind.

Back in the Peoples Temple Agricultural Project settlement, despite assurances from Congressman Leo Ryan prior to his departure that he would issue a report describing Jonestown "*in basically good terms*", Reverend Jim Jones mental state quickly deteriorated claiming to close Temple staff and ministry advisors that "*all was lost*" after 19-people in total had defected from the Temple.

Marceline Jones asked for everyone to return to their sleeping quarters and get some rest, all high-ranking Temple staff were called to the pavilion to meet with Jones.

Despite assurances that nothing much had changed Jones wasn't so sure and called another '*White Night*', a routine his followers were by now used to.

In a tape, often referred to as the '*death tape*', Reverend Jim Jones can be heard telling the gathering inside the pavilion "*one of those people on that plane is gonna shoot the pilot, I know that. I didn't plan it, but I know it's gonna happen. They're gonna shoot that pilot and down comes the plane into the jungle and we had better not have any of our children left when it's over, because they'll parachute in here on us."*

Jones went on to encourage the gathering to "commit revolutionary suicide" of which defectors and survivors recall it as the theory was "*you can go down in history, saying you chose your own way to go, and it is your commitment to refuse capitalism and in support of socialism.*"

While the '*death tape*' indicates at first there was hesitation from Temple member Christine Miller about exploring other options before taking the extraordinary step of revolutionary suicide, once the Red Brigade returned from the airstrip and confirmed to Reverend Jim Jones that the Congressman was dead, and it was announced to the congregation most objections ceased.

"The Congressman's dead," Jones told the congregation. *"Red Brigade showed them justice."*

According to escaped Temple member Odell Rhodes, the first to take the poison was Ruletta Paul and her one-year-old infant.

A syringe with its needle removed was filled and squirted into the mouth of first the infant, followed by Ruletta Paul.

Stanley Clayton also witnessed mothers with their babies first approach the tub containing the laced liquid.

Many of the members, after receiving their poisoned drink were led down the wooden walkway from the pavilion and to the grassed area that surrounded.

It is unknown how many, if any, thought that this was another case of a mock '*White Night*' scenario however, the poisoned drink had most members dead within five minutes of ingesting.

"*Die with a degree of dignity. Lay down your life with dignity; don't lay down with tears and agony.*" Jim Jones is heard to be preaching on the death tape.

"*I tell you, I don't care how many screams you hear, I don't care how many anguished cries...death is a million times preferable to 10 more days of this life. If you knew what was ahead of you – if you knew what was ahead of you, you'd be glad to be stepping over tonight.*"

Reverend Jim Jones was found dead laying in between two bodies next to his chair with a self-inflicted gunshot wound to his head.

918 people died, including 276 children and four who died at the Peoples Temple headquarters in Georgetown that same night.

The bodies of over 400 Peoples Temple members are buried in a mass-grave at Evergreen Cemetery in Oakland, California.

THE BRANCH DAVIDIANS

Vernon Howell (1959-1993), who later in life became David Koresh, taught that he was the last of a line of prophets, each with a specific "message" or revelation about the meaning of the Bible.

William Miller (1782-1849), whose interpretations resulted in a movement in the United States in which several dates were set for the return of Christ, the last of which was October 22, 1844 (termed the *"Great Disappointment"* by historians); Ellen G. White (1827-1915), the prophet who emerged out of the Millerite movement to reinterpret its failed prophecies, and around whom the Seventh-day Adventist Church coalesced; Victor T. Houteff (1885-1955), who split from the Seventh-day Adventist Church to establish the General Association of Davidian Seventh-Day Adventists ("Davidians") in Waco in 1935; Ben Roden (1902-1978), who emerged from the Davidians in 1955 to form the General Association of Branch Davidian Seventh-day Adventists ("Branch Davidians"), and who took over the remaining 77.86 acres of the Davidians' property named Mount Carmel on the outskirts of Waco, which Roden purchased on behalf of the Branch Davidian general association in 1973; and Lois Roden (1905-1986), Ben Roden's widow, who revealed to the Branch Davidians that the Holy Spirit is feminine.

Vernon Howell arrived at Mount Carmel in 1981 when he was twenty-two years old.

Thereafter Lois Roden gradually began to indicate he would succeed her as the next Branch Davidian prophet, and she took him to Israel several times.

Many followers and religious historians have stated that Roden's indications of Howell being the next Branch Davidian prophet came from a romantic and sexual relationship between the pair.

Roden and Howell claimed that it was 'Gods Plan' that they were to have a miracle child who would be the child of god, and the holy one anointed to become the future leader of the Branch Davidians.

However, in 1984 the core group of Branch Davidians at Mount Carmel concluded that Lois Roden had lost *"the Spirit of Prophecy*," and shifted their allegiance to Howell after Roden failed to conceive the announced Gods Childs.

They left Mount Carmel due to the violence of George Roden (1938-1998), Ben and Lois Roden's son, who wished to be the next Branch Davidian prophet controlling Mount Carmel.

The Branch Davidians moved to live with Vernon Howell and his new wife Rachel, first in rentals in Waco, then briefly in a rented camp at Mexia, Texas.

In 1985 Vernon and Rachel Howell visited Israel where he received his messianic calling.

In 1990 Vernon Howell legally changed his name to David Koresh, which expressed his identity as the Christ of the Last Days.

Koresh taught, and the Branch Davidians followers who had believed in him and left the Mount Carmel compound with him accepted, that he was more than a prophet, he embodied the Christ Spirit returned to be martyred, after which he would be resurrected as the leader of an army of 200 million martyrs of the ages (Rev. 9:16), including Branch Davidians martyred with him, to slay the wicked and create the Lord's Kingdom on the miraculously elevated and enlarged Mount Zion in the Holy Land.

The 200 million martyrs of the ages, as well as living persons who gave their all for David Koresh's message, are considered the "wave sheaf," the first of the "first fruits" of those offered to God, who will play elite roles in God's Kingdom.

Also, in 1985, the Branch Davidians settled in a camp they built on wooded property near Palestine, Texas.

They lived in school buses converted to housing, with a wooden cabin for cooking and meetings. Koresh often gave Bible studies in the open air.

He travelled frequently to California to proselytize and to promote his band.

His surviving recorded songs express his theological teachings.

He also travelled to Hawaii and Australia to proselytize. Several of the Branch Davidians travelled to California and Hawaii to work to support the community in Texas.

Branch Davidians in Texas worked at a variety of jobs, while women with children stayed at the camp. As converts began moving to the Palestine camp, they built small cottages in which to live.

Branch Davidians Sheila Martin, Catherine Matteson, and Bonnie Haldeman reported to Catherine Wessinger their fond memories of the communal life at the Palestine camp in the woods.

Most of the converts had Seventh-day Adventist backgrounds, some had conservative and/or Pentecostal Christian backgrounds, a few had left Catholicism on their quest to learn the truths contained in the Bible, and a few secular individuals were attracted to the message by the prospect of playing in Koresh's band.

In 1986 Koresh began taking additional wives with whom to have children to fulfil what he taught were the Bible's prophecies for the Christ of the Last Days to have twenty-four children, which he revealed to be the twenty-four elders next to the Lord's throne in the book of Revelation (4:4,10-11; 5:8; 14).

Teenagers as young as fourteen (the legal age at that time in Texas for a girl to marry, with parental consent) became Koresh's "wives" with permission of their parents.

One girl, Michele Jones, was twelve when she became Koresh's "wife." Girls and young women in the group were instructed that they would be Koresh's wives in the project of bearing messianic children.

Lois Roden died in 1986, which left George Roden in full control of Mount Carmel.

In 1987 George Roden dug up the casket of Anna Hughes, a Branch Davidian who was buried in the Mount Carmel cemetery almost twenty years earlier, he challenged Vernon Howell to see which one of them could raise her from the dead.

Howell reported the disinterment to the McLennan County Sheriff's Department, and, according to long-time supporter Clive Doyle, Howell was told that the deputies needed to see evidence that the body was exhumed before they would go to investigate.

Koresh and a group of Branch Davidian men armed themselves and went to Mount Carmel to photograph the body.

While there they got into a shootout with George Roden. Koresh and his men were arrested and charged with attempted murder. The trial of Vernon Howell (David Koresh) and the Branch Davidian men involved in the shootout with George Roden took place in Waco in 1988.

The jury could not come to a verdict on the charge against Howell, but all the other men were acquitted. Everyone was released from jail.

Howell had already paid bail and was released.

During the run-up to the trial, George Roden had written letters threatening God's punishment against the judge, so he was put into jail for contempt.

While he was in jail, Koresh took legal steps to reinstate a restraining order that had been taken out by Lois Roden to keep George Roden away from the Mount Carmel property and to prevent him from claiming to be the president of the General Association of Branch Davidian Seventh-day Adventists. (Despite the restraining order, Lois Roden had permitted George Roden to move back onto the property.)

When George Roden was released from jail he moved to Odessa, Texas, where in 1989 he killed a man.

George Roden was confined to the Big Spring State Hospital until his death in 1998.

In 1988 most of the Branch Davidians left the Palestine camp and moved back to Mount Carmel, where they cleaned up and repaired the little houses for living quarters.

They discovered equipment to make methamphetamine in one of the houses, which Koresh turned over to the Sheriff's Department.

In 1988 Steve Schneider, who had a Masters' degree in Religious Studies from the University of Hawaii, went to Britain to present Koresh's message to Adventists living near Newbold College, a Seventh-day Adventist institution.

Several British converts were gained from this trip and another one in 1990 by Schneider and from visits by David Koresh in 1988 or 1989.

By 1992 many of these Branch Davidians had joined the group living at Mount Carmel. In 1989 Koresh taught a "new light" revelation that all the women in the community (including already married women) were his wives with whom he could choose to have children, and all the men other than himself were to be celibate.

Marc Breault and his wife Elizabeth Baranyai left Mount Carmel and moved to Australia, where Breault worked to persuade Branch Davidians living in Australia and New Zealand that Koresh was a false prophet.

Breault began efforts to alert authorities in the United States about Koresh's activities, and he alerted Australian and Waco media to the "cult" at Mount Carmel whenever the opportunity arose.

In 1990, the year that Vernon Howell legally changed his name to David Koresh, Robyn Bunds left the Branch Davidians taking Shaun, her son with Koresh.

In 1991 Bunds filed a complaint with La Verne, California police that Koresh had taken Shaun to Mount Carmel.

After La Verne police officers visited Koresh at Mount Carmel, the leader promptly returned Shaun to his mother.

In 1991 Marc Breault alerted David Jewell in Michigan that his young daughter, Kiri Jewell (then aged ten) living at Mount Carmel with her mother Sherri Jewell, was slated to become one of Koresh's wives.

Breault flew to Michigan to testify in a custody hearing in which David Jewell gained full custody of Kiri and after which Sherri Jewell returned to Mount Carmel.

In 1992, in response to a complaint by David Jewell, social workers with the Texas Child Protective Services investigated Koresh.

Koresh permitted social worker Joyce Sparks to visit Mount Carmel and he explained his theology and teachings to her.

Sparks closed the case due to lack of evidence. Charges were not pressed against Koresh in relation to Kiri Jewell.

Also, in 1992 Dana Okimoto left the Branch Davidians with her two sons with Koresh, Sky and Scooter.

In the spring of 1992 the Branch Davidians moved into a large residence they had built at Mount Carmel, having demolished the small houses.

Many Branch Davidians came from England, Australia, and other locations in North America to Mount Carmel for that spring's Passover.

Marc Breault and other former Branch Davidians alleged to law enforcement and the media that the Branch Davidians would commit group suicide over Passover. Nothing happened.

By the end of 1992, overflights of helicopters and the arrival in the house across the street (Double EE Ranch Road) of a group of men claiming to be students, but who had carried in rifle cases, alerted Koresh and the Branch Davidians that they were under surveillance.

Nevertheless, in 1993 Koresh welcomed the men he knew to be undercover agents to Mount Carmel, shot AR- 15 semi-automatic rifles with them behind the building, gave Bible studies to one of them, Robert Rodriguez, inside the residence and invited him to move in.

Among the 124 Branch Davidians who were present at Mount Carmel during the ATF raid on February 28, 1993, 84 were Americans, 31 were British, five were Australians, two were Canadians, one was Israeli, and one was a New Zealander.

The community was multiracial. Of the British approximately 26 were Black, many of them with Jamaican family backgrounds.

There was one Nigerian Brit. There were eleven African Americans, eight Mexican Americans, and Americans of Japanese, Filipina, Chinese, Samoan, and mixed ethnicities.

There were 43 women (18 and older), 37 men (18 and older), and 44 children of all ages. Of the children, thirty were eight years old or younger. Twelve of the children were David Koresh's biological children.

Two young women were pregnant with Koresh's children: Nicole Gent (Australian, age 24) and Aisha Gyarfas Summers (Australian, age 17).

These figures do not include the Branch Davidians who were away from Mount Carmel on February 28.

On February 28, 1993, about 9:45 a.m., agents with the Bureau of Alcohol, Tobacco, and Firearms [ATF] pulled up at the front door of the residence at Mount Carmel in covered cattle trailers pulled by trucks to carry out a "no-knock" "dynamic entry" to deliver a search warrant and an arrest warrant for David Koresh.

The ATF's allegation was that the Branch Davidians, who had legally purchased forty AR-15 semi-automatic rifles, were converting them to M-16 automatic weapons without applying for the required license permits and paying the fees.

Alerted to the impending raid, an unarmed David Koresh met them at the front door saying words to the effect, *"Hey, wait a minute! There are women and children in here!"*

When shooting started, Koresh backed inside, the doors were shut, before ATF agents and Branch Davidians exchanged shots that pierced the metal double front doors.

Two teams of ATF agents used ladders to climb up to and enter second-floor windows of two rooms over the chapel, which they thought were Koresh's bedroom and Armory.

When the shootout erupted, Branch Davidian and Harvard-educated attorney Wayne Martin (American, age 42) dialled 911 from inside the compound, Martin reached Lieutenant Larry Lynch at the Sheriff's Department, and shouted into his speakerphone: *"There are seventy-five men around our building and they're shooting at us at Mount Carmel. Tell them there are children and women in here and to call it off!"*

In the shootout four ATF agents and five Branch Davidians were killed, twenty ATF agents were wounded, some severely, and four Branch Davidians were wounded, with David Koresh severely wounded by a bullet that pierced his side.

Later about 5:00 p.m. Branch Davidian Michael Schroeder was shot and killed by ATF agents as he attempted to walk back to Mount Carmel.

The ATF agents alleged that he shot at them first, despite no gun being found on or near the body of Schroeder.

A ceasefire at Mount Carmel was negotiated through the 911 call.

After ATF agents recovered their dead and wounded, they remained on alert at an armed perimeter around Mount Carmel until FBI agents took over the next day.

During the night and for several following days, some parents sent their children out.

Despite Koresh's wounds, he immediately began giving telephone interviews to CNN and radio talk shows in Texas explaining his theology, and he negotiated with ATF agent James Cavanaugh and Lieutenant Larry Lynch.

Koresh insisted to Lynch the significance of his theology for the unfolding events: *"Look, this is life, this is life and death...theology really is life and death."* Because of the deaths of federal agents, FBI agents took control of Mount Carmel on March 1 and gave the case the internal code WACMUR (Waco Murder).

FBI agents took over the negotiations and the FBI's elite Hostage Rescue Team (HRT) commanded by Dick Rogers brought in its snipers and on March 2nd brought in tanks.

Jeffrey Jamar from the San Antonio, Texas FBI office was the Special Agent in Charge of the WACMUR case.

Bob Ricks of the Oklahoma City, Oklahoma office was the FBI agent who spoke most often at press briefings. Gary Noesner from the FBI's Special Operations and Research Unit at Quantico, Virginia, was negotiation coordinator from March 1st to March 24th; before Clint Van Zandt became negotiation coordinator from March 25th to April 19th, 1993.

Byron Sage was the FBI agent from Austin, Texas, who was the first to arrive to assist Lieutenant Larry Lynch with negotiations on February 28th, and he continued to play key roles in the negotiations through to the devastating conclusion on April 19th.

Throughout the siege the FBI negotiators, commanders, Special Agents in Charge in Waco were in constant contact with FBI officials in the Strategic Information and Operations Centre (SIOC) in the Hoover Building in Washington, D.C.

According to the FBI WACMUR Major Event Log available in the Lee Hancock Collection in the Southwestern Writers Collection at Texas State University-San Marcos, the officials in SIOC to whom agents in Waco most often reported were: Danny Coulson, Deputy Assistant Director and former commander of the HRT; Larry Potts, Assistant Director; and E. Michael Kahoe, Chief of the Violent Crimes and Major Offenders Section.

These officials reported to Deputy Director Floyd I. Clarke and Director William S. Sessions.

On March 1st, the FBI cut off Koresh's telephone line to the outside world, thereby preventing him from talking to the media. Koresh then negotiated that he would surrender after his audiotaped sermon presenting his theology was broadcast on the Christian Broadcasting Network and the radio.

The audiotape was brought out by Catherine Matteson (American, age 77) on the morning of March 2nd.

The tape was duly played, the Branch Davidians prepared to carry Koresh out on a stretcher, but at the last-minute Koresh reported that God had told him that they should wait.

Steve Schneider, David Koresh' right hand man spoke most often to negotiators during the siege, explained that just as the agents had their commander, Koresh had his commander and he had to wait on orders.

During negotiations conducted first by Lieutenant Larry Lynch, then concurrently by Lynch with Sage assisting and James Cavanaugh of the ATF, and later by FBI negotiators under the supervision of Gary Noesner, twenty-one children were sent out.

During the period of Noesner's supervision of negotiations fourteen adults came out.

However, every time Branch Davidian members came out the remaining members inside the Mount Carmel compound were punished by actions taken by the Hostage Rescue Team.

Beginning on March 9th when the HRT cut the building's electricity off which Noesner says in his book, Stalling for Time (2010), he informed Special Agent in Charge Jeffrey Jamar only served to aggravate the Branch Davidians.

Noesner reports that on March 11th additional Bradley tanks and M1 Abrams tanks were brought to Mount Carmel, the latter of which Jamar proclaimed, to the dismay of the negotiators, could drive straight through the building.

On March 12th two adults came out, but the HRT then cut off the electricity to the compound for the final time, angering David Koresh and Steve Schneider.

On March 15th Schneider and Wayne Martin stood outside the building to negotiate with McLennan County Sheriff Jack Harwell and FBI agent Byron Sage, where a recording later in the day captures David Koresh sending a CB message to the FBI agents thanking them for being cordial in the face-to-face talk:

"Let everybody just rest assured that you act decent, so we're going to act decent and we're all human beings, and we're all under God, and under this country. Let's see if we can't work this out. Let's don't get itchy. We won't get itchy. Let's just relax and think about mamas and papas and babies…."

On the same day Steve Schneider reported to negotiators that the Branch Davidians had heard Bible scholar Dr. J. Phillip Arnold of Houston on the radio discussing the Bible's prophecies, and he asked that Dr. Arnold be permitted to discuss the prophecies with David Koresh, the request was never granted.

On March 21st seven Davidian adults came out, but the HRT then used tanks to crush and remove some of the Branch Davidians' vehicles, angering the Branch Davidians. Noesner reports that he protested this action to Jamar to no avail.

Noesner also tried to persuade Jamar not to permit implementation of the plan to blast irritating, high-decibel sounds toward the Branch Davidians.

The loud sounds were initiated that evening, and Steve Schneider informed negotiators that the Branch Davidians who had intended to come out had decided to stay inside.

On March 23rd Livingstone Fagan, a Branch Davidian from England with a Seventh-day Adventist Master of Divinity degree, was sent out to explain Koresh's theology to the agents.

He was the last adult to come out before the April 19th final assault on the compound.

After Clint Van Zandt took over as FBI negotiation coordinator on March 25th, he and the FBI negotiators had to contend with the aggressive actions carried out by the Hostage Rescue Team with the approval of officials in SIOC in Washington, D.C., as evidenced in the WACMUR Major Event Log.

On March 29th, 30th, and 31st, Dick DeGuerin, an attorney from Houston who had agreed to represent David Koresh, went inside the building for discussions with his client.

Jack Zimmerman, who had agreed to be Steve Schneider's attorney, went inside the building with DeGuerin on April 1st.

Gradually after their visits, David Koresh, who had probably been suffering from infection (the FBI WACMUR Major Event

Log records that Steve Schneider frequently expressed this concern to negotiators), began to be awake for longer periods and speak more often to negotiators, making it likely that the attorneys took antibiotics into the compound during their visits.

On April 2nd Schneider informed negotiators that they would come out after the eight days of Passover.

The FBI WACMUR Major Event Log reports some uncertainty on the part of the Branch Davidians in calculating the beginning day for Passover. Eventually they settled on Monday, April 5th.

On April 4th DeGuerin and Zimmerman took inside an audiotape of Dr. J. Phillip Arnold and Dr. James D. Tabor, University of North Carolina, Charlotte, discussing alternative interpretations of the book of Revelation on an April 1st radio program.

Upon exiting the compound after a visit with their clients, DeGuerin and Zimmerman told FBI agents that the Branch Davidians would come out after Passover, which began the next day.

They also told a reporter with the New York Times that they had observed incoming bullet holes in the topmost ceiling of the building the four-story central tower and that the Branch Davidians alleged that ATF agents had shot at the building from National Guard helicopters on February 28th.

DeGuerin and Zimmerman expressed concern that the tanks crushing and moving vehicles were destroying evidence. This story appeared in the New York Times on April 5th ("Sect's Lawyers Dispute Gunfight Details").

During Passover week Steve Schneider complained to negotiators about the high decibel sounds as being disrespectful of their sacred time, but the WACMUR Major Event Log indicates that the sounds continued to be played throughout the night.

Beginning on April 7th HRT agents began firing flash-bang grenades at Branch Davidians who came outside the building to collect rainwater in the courtyard or to get some fresh air, something they had previously been granted permission to do.

On April 9th, Good Friday, Steve Schneider obtained permission to go outside and light seven smoke canisters in honour of Christ's death.

The Major Event Log records that later that evening an HRT agent reported to SIOC that per SAC Jamar and HRT-ASAC Rogers *"there would be no plan to fight a fire should one develop in the Davidian compound."*

An hour later Steve Schneider called the negotiators *"absolutely distraught"* over being flash-banged after agents in a tank beckoned to him to come outside.

He went outside because it had become customary for the tanks to drop off items for Branch Davidians to take inside.

On Wednesday, April 14th, the day after the conclusion of Passover, DeGuerin and Zimmerman spoke with Koresh and Schneider by telephone, who read them a letter from Koresh saying they would come out after he wrote a "little book" explaining his interpretations of the Seven Seals of Revelation and the manuscript was given to Drs. Arnold and Tabor for safekeeping and dissemination.

That afternoon, as reported in the Major Event Log, a series of banners was hung out from tower windows: *"Read Proverbs 1, 2, 3, 4. We come to love not war." "Let's have a beer when this is over." "My name is Neil Vaega. I'm from Hawaii."*

That evening at 7:45 p.m. David Koresh sent out the contract he had signed to retain DeGuerin as his attorney in addition to his letter outlining his exit plan that had been read over the telephone earlier that day.

The Major Event Log records that on April 16th at 1:15 a.m. a Bradley tank rammed the outside wall of one of the bedrooms, almost injuring Australian believer Graeme Craddock who was sleeping in a bunk there.

Nevertheless, Koresh reported at 2:35 a.m. that he had completed his commentary on the First Seal.

He reiterated that he was working day and night on the manuscript and that they would come out when it was completed.

Branch Davidians began requesting batteries and ribbon cassettes for a battery-operated word-processor to facilitate faster production of the manuscript.

According to the United States Department of Justice, Report to the Deputy Attorney General on the Events at Waco, Texas, February 28th to April 19th, 1993, on April 12th the FBI began persuading Attorney General Janet Reno to approve a plan to gas the building to drive the Branch Davidians out.

Reno was new to Washington, having been sworn in as Attorney General in the new Bill Clinton Administration on March 12th, 1993, after the siege at Mount Carmel had begun.

On April 12th Reno was dubious of the proposed plan to insert gas into the building. On April 14th FBI officials brought in Dr. Harry Salem, a U.S. Army research toxicologist, to assuage Reno's concerns about the harmful effects of CS gas.

Dick Rogers, HRT commander, told Reno that negotiations with the Branch Davidians had broken down.

Reno continued to ask why an assault was needed at that time. A telephone call, which lasted for two hours, was set up between Acting Associate Attorney General Webster Hubbell and Supervisory Special Resident Agent Byron Sage on April 15th to discuss the state of negotiations with the Branch Davidians.

According to the Report to the Deputy Attorney General and Sage's congressional testimony in 1995, Sage told Hubbell that negotiations with David Koresh and the Branch Davidians were at an impasse, and that negotiators would never be able to persuade Koresh to come out or to send others out.

Hubbell reported this information to Reno.

Shortly after Hubbell conveyed to the FBI on April 16th that Reno still declined to approve the plan, FBI Director William S. Sessions, Deputy Director Floyd I. Clarke, and Assistant Director Larry Potts arrived in Hubbell's office and asked to speak to Reno.

Reno requested that documentation relating to the proposed plan be prepared for her to examine on the following day.

According to the Major Event Log, on Saturday, April 17 at 5:00 p.m., Sessions, Clarke, and Potts briefed Attorney General Janet Reno on the "proposed operational plan."

The Major Event Log records that by 7:00 p.m. Reno had approved the plan and it would be implemented on Monday, April 19th.

Attorney General Reno's authorised for the FBI tank and CS gas assault on the Branch Davidians. The first sixty-seven pages of documents in the Briefing File relate to allegations of Koresh's abuse of children, including a memo from psychiatrist Park Dietz stating it was likely that Koresh was continuing to abuse children sexually during the siege, an assertion that Reno made to the press immediately after the fire, which she had to retract as not being supported by any gathered evidence.

The memo dated March 5th, 1993, by FBI psychological profilers Pete Smerick and Mark C. Young, is effectively buried on pages 74- 76 of the a highly sourced document nicknamed the 'Reno Briefing File'.

This memo explains that David Koresh had taught and that his followers believed that they would die in an attack by federal agents.

They counselled a low-key tactical presence, noting that children had been sent out during periods when the tanks were pulled back.

They pointed out that aggressive actions against the Branch Davidians served to confirm Koresh's apocalyptic prophecies: "If these forces continue to move closer to the compound, the increased paranoia of these people could result in their firing weapons, thus encouraging retaliation, leading to an escalation of violence."

Two crucial memos by Smerick and Young, dated March 7th and 8th, 1993, are not included in the "Reno Briefing File."

The March 7th, 1993, memo recommended continued negotiations with the assistance of Sheriff Jack Harwell, who was highly respected by the Branch Davidians.

If the Mount Carmel compound was to be attacked, in all probability, David Koresh and his followers will fight back to the death, to defend their property and their faith, as they believe they did on February 28th, 1993.

If that occurs, there would have to be an HRT response and the possibility of a tremendous loss of life, both within the compound, and of Bureau personnel.

Commanders are thus faced with the prospect of defending their actions and justifying the taking of lives of children, who are with their families in a *"defensive position"*, defending their religion, regardless of how bizarre and cult like we believe it is manifested.

Smerick and Young's March 8th, 1993 memo advises that the Branch Davidians saw Mount Carmel as sacred ground, and that he and his followers would die fighting to defend it.

"It should not be overlooked that [Koresh] is a religious fanatic with delusions of being JESUS CHRIST, and that he and his followers will die as a result of being attacked by his enemies."

Smerick and Young inaccurately discuss Koresh's interpretations of the Seven Seals of Revelation, but they correctly grasp that Koresh's prediction was that some Branch Davidians would die in a conflict with federal agents as had happened on February 28th and after a period the rest of them would die in an assault. (*This was Koresh's interpretation of the Fifth Seal.*)

Smerick and Young write: In traditional hostage negotiations with people who are psychopaths, the goal is to wrest control away from the individual and give him a face-saving scenario, so he can surrender.

With David Koresh, however, perhaps one way to take control away from him is to do the **OPPOSITE** of what he is expecting.

Instead of moving towards him, we consider moving back. This may appear to be appeasement to his wishes, but, it is taking power away from him.

He has told his followers that an attack is imminent, and this will show them that he was wrong. Smerick and Young's March 8th, 1993 memo warned that Koresh might order a *"mass suicide"* if his status as the group's messiah was threatened.

These two memos by Smerick and Young are not in the *"Reno Briefing File,"* but their memo of March 9th, 1993, advocating hard-line measures *"to break the spirit"* of Koresh is found on pages 82-83 of the file.

Lee Hancock's Dallas Morning News article of March 6th, 2000 reports Smerick telling her that the memo dated March 9th, 1993 was written under pressure from officials in Washington.

On pages 163-68 of the *"Reno Briefing File"* is a summary of British studies alleging that CS *"riot control agent"* is not harmful to children and unborn foetuses as-long-as they are removed quickly from the gassed area.

According to David B. Kopel and Paul H. Blackman, No More Wacos (1997), this document does not report that a baby exposed to CS in a home in Northern Ireland spent twenty-eight days in a hospital receiving medical intervention before recovering.

The last document in the file is the proposed operation plan for the assault (pages 169- 77). Plan A approved by Reno allowed for the gradual insertion of CS gas into the building over forty-eight hours in the hope that the parents would bring their children out.

It contained a provision that the FBI commanders on the ground could switch to Plan B, the rapid insertion of CS, if FBI agents received gunfire from the Branch Davidians.

Plan B was put into operation within a few minutes after the final assault started on April 19th.

On April 18th before 2:00 p.m. the remaining Branch Davidian vehicles parked around the residence were crushed and removed by tanks (Combat Engineering Vehicles).

A transcript of a negotiation audiotape made by Catherine Wessinger included in How the Millennium Comes Violently (2000) shows that Koresh called a negotiator and asked, *"what do you men really want?"* Koresh warned: *"These commanders are fixing to ruin the safety of me and my children. My life, the lives of my wives, the lives of my friends, my family. You are fixing to step across the ribbon."*

He explained that the tactical actions were cornering him: *"If this is the corner of the box that you place me in to...."* The audiotape was cut off when Koresh and the negotiator got into a shouting match.

Nevertheless, Steve Schneider continued to ask for word-processing supplies and these were delivered by 9:30 p.m.

On April 19th, 1993 at 6:00 a.m. the FBI's Hostage Rescue Team initiated a tank and CS gas assault against the building.

FBI officials in SIOC in Washington watched the assault on closed circuit television. The Updated Event Log for April 19th, 1993 and information given by retired Colonel Rodney Rawlings of the United States Army to Lee Hancock of the Dallas Morning News in 1999 together indicate that officials in SIOC and FBI Special Agents in Charge and other agents near Mount Carmel listened in real time to audio captured by surveillance devices inside the building.

(After the fire, the FBI alleged that agents were not listening in real time to audio captured by bugs on April 18th and 19th, so they did not hear the Branch Davidians' discussions of an imminent fire and fulfillment of prophecies on April 18th, and discussions of pouring fuel on the morning of April 19th.)

The Updated Event Log for April 19th, 1993 in the Lee Hancock Collection indicates that FBI officials in SIOC and the FBI commanders in Waco were in constant contact during the assault.

Throughout the assault Byron Sage announced through the loudspeaker, *"This is not an assault,"* and called for the Branch Davidians to surrender.

Grenade launchers were used to fire in small rocket-shaped ferret rounds to release the gas, and CS was inserted through sprayers attached to the booms of Combat Engineering Vehicles.

Four hundred ferret rounds were fired within the first hour, and additional rounds were brought in. Instead of coming out, the Branch Davidian adults put on gas masks and attempted to dodge the tanks when they penetrated the building.

There were no child-sized gas masks.

Survivor Derek Lovelock reports in "A Personal View" (2006): The gas masks that we had were not small enough for some of the children, so we drenched towels in water and wrapped them around the children's heads and then put the masks over them.

There were some little children as young as three and they were crying and coughing with tears streaming down their faces as they struggled to breathe.

According to Lovelock, *"The gas masks that we had would last about half an hour before they started to fail. When they do, you can feel the gas getting to you and your eyes begin to burn."*

The small children and their mothers took shelter in a concrete vault located at the base of the central tower, the door to which had been removed when a large refrigerator had been put into that space.

The open doorway to the vault faced out toward the front of the building.

According to the analysis of FBI audio and video recorded on April 19th, 1993 by attorney David Hardy in This Is Not an Assault (2001), a tank drove into the building and from 11:31 a.m. to 11:55 a.m. gassed the area of the vault's open doorway.

Then the tank backed out of the building and moved to the southeast front corner of the building to use its boom to penetrate the outer wall of the second-floor room.

Hardy argues that this is where David Koresh and Steve Schneider were located.

At the same time, a tank began driving through the gymnasium heading toward that same part of the building.

At 12:01 p.m. Byron Sage announced over the loudspeaker: *"David, we are facilitating you leaving the compound by enlarging the door. David, you have had your fifteen minutes of fame…. Vernon is no longer the messiah."*

The two tanks backed out of the building, and a fire became visible in the southeast corner second-floor bedroom window at 12:07 p.m. FLIR [Forward Looking Infrared] footage shot from a Nightstalker aircraft (according to the Major Event Log it was provided by Westinghouse) circling over Mount Carmel shows that at 12:08 and 12:09 p.m. fires were apparent in the cafeteria, the chapel, and the gymnasium.

Fire quickly engulfed the building and produced a huge fireball explosion.

Fifty-three adults and twenty-three children, including two infants born during the assault, died. Nine people escaped the fire, some badly burned.

Branch Davidian survivors include the nine people who escaped the fire, people who came out during the siege, and other people who were not at Mount Carmel on February 28th, 1993 when the ATF raid initiated the siege.

Twenty-five years after the incident debate still rages surrounding David Koresh and the Branch Davidians. These debates included who fired the first shots during the siege at the Mount Carmel compound, and the hotly debated topic of who started the fires which eventually engulfed the compound.

The stance from the United States Government is that it was David Koresh who led the agents of the Alcohol, Tobacco and Firearms into an ambush with members of the Branch Davidians lying in wait within the compound awaiting their arrival.

Surviving members of the Branch Davidians allege that David Koresh was unarmed, and that ATF Agents fired the first shots, however remain divided as to whether the shots were fired towards their religious leader or the guard dogs whose kennels were a short distance from the front door.

Survivor Kevin Jones – who was a child who left the Mount Carmel compound during the 51-day siege and was the second last child to be taken by authorities after he was asked by his aunty inside the property if he wanted to leave.

Jones states *"Anyone who wanted to leave could have just walked out the front door,"* further adding to the wide known fact that compound-based religious members were confined to the property due to sheer terror of the tactics implemented by the Federal Bureau of Investigation and their agents.

Kevin explains that on the morning the raid began everything happened so quickly, his father was tipped off in relation to the impending raid less than an hour before the cattle trucks filled with Alcohol, Tobacco and Firearms agents approached the main building of the Mount Carmel compound.

Despite the animosity that exists between surviving Branch Davidians and the Government of the United States of America, Kevin Jones says he as a child he was treated very well after leaving the compound.

"We were all treated very well. I was taken to an airplane hangar and fed from a vending machine, I was then given a sleeping bag and took a nap."

"I talked to my aunt on the telephone, and even answered questions in a room full of reporters. Then I was taken to the Methodist Home and reunited with the other children that had left during the siege."

Kevin further explains however that not everything was rosy upon leaving the compound.

"I was pat searched before entering the tank they picked me up in. They took my bag of clothes and teddy bear away and never returned them – even to this day."

As a young Kevin Jones left the compound David Koresh was laying the hallway, seriously injured from the gunshot he had suffered during the opening exchanges of the siege.

He was weak and growing weaker with every day that passed, he was moved into a nearby room to ease the concerns of Branch Davidian followers and compound members.

He was struggling to breath, in pain, and was in absolutely no position to refrain anyone from leaving.

Putting to bed the notion that he prevented the parents of the children who perished in the fire from leaving.

Kevin Jones further believes that is was the United States of America Government who started the fire that killed the remaining religious supporters inside the Mount Carmel Compound.

After the government cut off the electricity the Branch Davidians were forced to resort to using Kerosene lamps to light the hallways and bedrooms.

With the tear gas fired into the buildings, which burns at more than 1000 degrees, it, to Kevin and many sleuths around the world believe, could have easily knocked the lamps over setting the wooden structure alight.

MANSON FAMILY

It was the roaring sixties, the youth across America were divided, you were either a fighter in Vietnam - a war most of the country was against - or you were a lover, a free spirit, aimed at protesting the governments involvement in the War and living life to its fullest.

But there were a few that were lost souls, ones that were somewhere in between and confused as to where they stood, and where they belonged in the whole scheme of things.

Many of the lost souls joined the love movement and headed to California on the West Coast of the United States, with popular music groups such as the Beach Boys playing throughout the beachside diners, and nationwide advertising promoting the image of Californians being laid-back, tanned beach-goers it was no surprise that it soon became the 'go-to' place for the youth movement that wanted to stand up to an oppressive government.

The youth from across America, who had embraced the term hippie, created their own communities, listened to psychedelic music, embraced the sexual revolution, with many using drugs such as marijuana, LSD, peyote and psilocybin mushrooms to explore altered states of consciousness.

Some sought guidance, a purpose, a reason... and so when a charismatic Charles Manson, born Charles Milles Maddox, opened the door for the lost souls to learn the word of god, while living in a quasi-communal environment with others in a similar position it was no surprise that many took the opportunity available to them and joined the group that would become known worldwide as "The Manson Family".

Born to unmarried 16-year-old Kathleen Manson-Bower-Cavender, nee Maddox (1918-1973) at the General Hospital in Cincinnati, Ohio the baby originally named "no name Maddox" within weeks was called Charles Milles Maddox.

Manson's biological father appears to have been Colonel Walker Henderson Scott Sr. (1910 – 1954) who worked intermittently in local mills and had a local reputation as a con artist.

He allowed Kathleen Maddox to believe that he was an army colonel, although "Colonel" was merely his given name. The story worked well for him when Maddox told him she was pregnant, he informed her that he had been called away on army business; after several months of no contact Maddox began to realise he had no intention of returning.

In August 1934, prior to the birth of Charles, Maddox married William Eugene Manson (1909 – 1961), whose occupation was listed on Charles' birth certificate as a "labourer" at a dry-cleaning business. Maddox went on drinking sprees for days at a time with her brother, Luther, leaving a baby Charles with a variety of babysitters.

In August of 1934, just a few years after Maddox' divorce from Manson was approved by a court she and Luther's girlfriend, Julia Vickers, spent the evening drinking with a new acquaintance, Frank Martin, who appeared to be wealthy.

Maddox and Vickers decided to rob him, and Maddox phoned her brother to help.

They were incompetent thieves and were found and arrested within hours. At a trial seven weeks later, Luther was sentenced to ten years in prison, and Kathleen was sentenced to five years.

Charles Manson was placed in the home of an aunt and uncle in McMechen, West Virginia. His mother was paroled in 1942, Charles Manson would later characterize the first weeks after she returned from prison as the happiest time in his life.

Following her release from prison the family moved to Charleston, where Manson played would continuously play truant and his mother spent evening drinking. She was arrested for grand larceny, but not convicted.

After moving to Indianapolis, Maddox started Alcoholic Anonymous meetings, where she met an alcoholic name Lewis, whom she married in August 1943.

As well as constantly playing truant, Manson began stealing from stores and from his home. In 1957, Maddox looked for a temporary foster home for Manson. But she was unable to find a suitable one.

Instead she decided to send him to the Gibault School for Boys in Terre Haute, Indiana, a school for male delinquents run by Catholic priests. Manson soon fled home to his mother, but she took him back to the school.

Manson returned to Gibault after he spent Christmas of 1947 in McMechen at the house of his aunt and uncle, where he was caught stealing a gun.

He again ran away from the Gibault School but instead of returning to his mother, where he was afraid that she would return him to the school, he began to support himself by burglarizing stores and night and renting a room.

Eventually he was caught, and a sympathetic judge sent him to Boys Town, a juvenile facility in Omaha, Nebraska. After four days, he and a student named Blackie Nielson stole a car and somehow obtained a gun, which they used to rob a grocery store and a casino, as they made their way to the home of Neilson's uncle in Peoria, Illinois.

Neilson's uncle was a professional thief, and when the boys arrived he apparently took them on as apprentices. During the second of two subsequent break-ins of grocery stores, Manson was arrested and sent at age 13 to the Indiana Boys School, a strict "reform school" where he later claimed that he was raped by other students with the encouragement of a staff member.

Manson as a result developed a self-defence technique he later called the "insane game", in which he would screech, grimace and wave his arms to convince aggressors that he was insane when he was physically unable to defend himself.

After many failed attempts to break out of the juvenile correctional facility, he escaped with two other boys in 1851.

The three escapees were attempting to drive to California in stolen cars when they were arrested in Utah.

They had robbed several filling stations along the way, driving a stolen car across state lines is a federal crime that violates the Dyer Act. Manson was sent to Washington D. C's National Training School for Boys.

On arrival he was given aptitude tests, he was illiterate, and his IQ was 109 – where the national average was 100. His case worker deemed him aggressively antisocial.

Following a psychiatrist's recommendation, Manson was transferred in October 1951 to Natural Bridge Honour Camp, a minimum-security institution.

His aunt visited him and told administrators she would let him stay at her house as well as help him find work. Manson has a parole hearing scheduled for February 1952, however, in January, he was caught raping a boy at knifepoint.

Manson was immediately transferred to the Federal Reformatory in Petersburg, Virginia, where he committed a further "eight serious disciplinary offenses, three involving homosexual acts", as a result he was sent to a maximum-security reformatory at Chillicothe, Ohio, where he was expected to stay until his release on his 21st birthday in November 1955.

Good behaviour led to an early release in May 1954, to live with his aunt and uncle in McMechen.

In January 1955 Manson married a hospital waitress named Rosalie Jean Willie, around October, about three months after he and his pregnant wife arrived in Los Angeles in a car he had stolen in Ohio, Manson was again charged with a federal crime for taking the vehicle across state lines.

After a psychiatric evaluation he was given five years' probation. Manson's subsequent failure to appear at a Los Angeles hearing on an identical charge filed in Florida resulted in his March 1956 arrest in Indianapolis.

His probation was revoked, and he was sentenced to three years' imprisonment at Terminal Island, San Pedro in California.

While Manson was in prison, Rosalie gave birth to their son Charles Manson, Jr. During his first year at Terminal Island, Manson received visits from Rosalie and his mother, who were now living together in Los Angeles.

However, in March 1957 his visits from his wife ceased. Manson's' mother informed him Rosalie was living with another man. Less than two weeks before a scheduled parole hearing, Manson tried to escape by stealing a car.

He was subsequently given five years' probation, and his parole was denied.

In September 1958 Manson received five years' parole, the same year in which his wife Rosalie received a decree of divorce.

By November he was pimping a 16-year-old girl and was receiving additional support from a girl with wealthy parents. In September 1959, he pleaded guilty to a charge of attempting to cash a forged U.S Treasury check, which he claimed to have stolen from a mailbox; the latter charge was later dropped.

He received a 10-year suspended sentence and probation after a young woman name Leona, who had an arrest record for prostitution, made a *"tearful plea"* before the court saying that she and Manson were *"deeply in love ... and would marry if Charlie were freed."*

Before the year's end, the woman did marry Manson, although it is widely thought this marriage was so testimony against him would not be required of her.

Leona was taken to New Mexico along with another woman by Manson for the purposes of prostitution, resulting in Manson being held and questioned for violation of the Mann Act.

The Mann Act is a federal law in the United States of America passed on June 25th, 1910 which in its original form made it a felony to engage in interstate or foreign commerce transport of "any woman or girl for the purpose of prostitution or debauchery, or for any other immoral purpose."

Its primary stated intent was to address prostitution, immorality, and human trafficking, particularly where trafficking was for the purposes of prostitution.

Although he was released, Manson correctly suspected that the investigation had not ended and when he disappeared in violation of his probation, a bench warrant was issued.

An indictment for violation of the Mann Act followed in April of 1960. When one of the woman was arrested for prostitution, Manson was arrested in June in Laredo, Texas and was returned to Los Angeles. For violation of his probation on the check-cashing charge, he was ordered to serve his ten-year sentence.

Manson spent a year unsuccessfully trying to appeal the revocation of his probation. In July 1961, he was transferred from Los Angeles County Jail to the United States Penitentiary at McNeil Island, Washington.

There, he took guitar lessons from Barker-Karpis gang leader Alvin "Creepy" Karpis and obtained the contact information of Gary Stromberg at Universal Studios in Hollywood from another inmate, music producer Phil Kaufman.

Kaufman thought Manson was a very bad guitar player, but capable enough as a singer and songwriter to have a chance of getting a record contract.

He advised Manson that upon his release to wait a few months to give him a chance to acclimatize to the outside world, do some work on his songs, then used the most polished compositions to showcase his potential when he went to see the music producer acquaintance of Kaufman's.

Manson, who Kaufman believed was self-obsessed, promised to take the advice.

By the time of Manson's release day, he had spent more than half of his 32 years in prisons and other institutions and even requested permission to stay in jail when authorities came to collect him for release, begging and protesting that prison had become his home.

Months after his release, by which time he had acquired the first four of his female devotees, Manson went to see Stromberg.

On the strength of the recommendation from Kaufman, the producer authorized a studio recording session. Instead of having been prepared as Kaufman had advised during his time incarcerated, with a few his best songs, Manson was unfocused and amateurish making the recording a disappointment.

It was Friday 8th August 1969, Hollywood starlet Sharon Tate called friends that she had previously invited for the evening and stated that she was not feeling well and was going to remain home – cancelling the invite.

Abigail Folger and Wojiciech Frykowski, two friends that had been living in her home since March 1969, were also home at the time.

In her final phone call to friends Sharon Tate stated that Jay Sebring, her one-time fiancé, would probably drop over later in the evening.

Sharon Tate had been with her husband, film producer-director, Roman Polanski, in London, England from March 1969 until approximately July 21, 1969, when she returned home to the property they leased at 10050 Cielo Drive.

Her husband, Roman, was to remain in Europe and return to California on August 12.

In addition to the house that the Polanski's leased, which was located at the centre of the Cielo property, the owner of the property, Rudy Autabelli, had his home at the very southernmost portion of the grounds.

Autabelli had left his house and several dogs in the care of William Garretson, his houseboy. Garretson's only duties were to care for the dogs and keep Autabelli's home in good order.

The main house leased by the Polanski's were their own responsibility as to the maintenance and domestic help.

Garretson was visited by his friend Steven Parent from 2345 on the 8th of August until quarter-past-twelve in the morning on the 9th.

The 10050 Cielo Drive property was not new territory for those about to become notorious with evil. On March 23, 1969 Charles Manson entered the property, uninvited, a place he knew as the property of Terry Melcher of whom he had met through Beach Boy Dennis Wilson.

Manson had gone to the property to confront Melcher who was meant to visit The Family at Spahn Ranch to hear material that members of The Family had recorded, the women of the group had prepared a meal and cleaned the place, but Melcher never arrived.

Wanting to confront the music executive Manson went to his last known address, 10050 Cielo Drive, where he was confronted by Shahrokh Hatami, an Iranian photographer and a friend of Sharon Tate, who was there to photograph Tate in advance of her departure for Rome the following day.

Hatami had seen Manson through a window as he approached the main house. Shahrokh Hatami had gone onto the front porch to ask the stranger what he wanted.

When Manson told Hatami he was looking for someone whose name Hatami did not recognize he was informed that this was the Polanski residence.

Manson was advised to try "the back alley", by which he meant the path to the guest house, beyond the main residence.

Appearing behind Hatami in the front door of the house was actress Sharon Tate who asked who was calling. Hatami said a man was looking for someone, they maintained their positions while Charles Manson without a word went back to the guest house, returned a minute or two later and left.

Later that evening Charles Manson returned to the property and again went back to the guest house, presuming to enter the enclosed porch he spoke with Rudi Altobelli who was just coming out of the shower.

Altobelli felt that Charles Manson had come to look for him, a fact backed up by prosecutor Vincent Bugliosi's discovery that Manson had apparently been to the place on earlier occasions after Melcher's departure from it.

Speaking through the inner screen door, Altobelli told Manson that Melcher had moved to Malibu. He then lied to Charles Manson and said that he did not know Melcher's new address.

In response to a question posed by Manson, Altobelli said he was in the entertainment business, although, having met Manson the previous year, at the home of Beach Boy Dennis Wilson, he was sure that Manson already knew that.

When Altobelli informed Manson he was going out of the country the next day, Charles Manson said he'd like to speak with him upon his return. Altobelli then lied again and said that he would be gone for more than a year.

In response to a direct question from Altobelli, Manson explained that he had been directed to the guest house by the persons in the main house, Altobelli expressed to Manson his desire that he not disturb his tenants.

Manson left and as Altobelli flew with Tate to Rome the next day the actress asked him whether "that creepy-looking guy" had gone back to the guest house the day before.

It was just before midnight when Tex Watson, Susan Atkins, Linda Kasabian and Patricia Krenwinkel arrived at the 10050 Cielo Drive address from Spahn Ranch.

The females had the strict instructions by the leader of the family Charles Manson to do as Watson would instruct. As they prepared to carry out their heinous crime that would have the entire group forever associated with evil Tex Watson had told them to "*totally destroy everyone in it, as gruesome as you can.*"

Tex Watson, who had been to the property before after previously driving Manson in his hunt a few months earlier for music executive Terry Melcher who had originally been keen to sign Manson to a recording contract only to get cold feet and back out, climbed a telephone pole near the entrance gate and cut the phone line to prevent telephone access to the house.

The group backed their car to the bottom of the hill that led to the estate, parked, and walked back up to the house. Thinking that the gate may be electrified or rigged with an alarm they climbed a brushy embankment to the right of the gate and dropped onto the grounds.

By this point it was just after midnight on August 9th, 1969.

Headlights approached them from father within the angled property, Tex Watson ordered the women to lie in the bushes to hide while he stepped out and ordered the approaching driver to halt.

18-year-old student Steven Parent who had been visiting the property's caretaker William Garretson, who was living in the properties guesthouse.

Watson levelled a 22-caliber revolver at Parent, the terrified youth begged Watson not to hurt him, claiming that he wouldn't say anything.

Tex Watson first lunged at Parent with a knife, giving him a defensive slash on the palm of his hands, severing tendons and tearing the boy's watch off his wrist, then shot the 18-year-old four times in the chest and abdomen – killing him.

Following the death of Steven Parent, Tex Watson had Linda Kasabian search around the main house for an open window, which she soon found and pointed it out to Watson.

Tex Watson then cut the screen to the window identified by Kasabian as being open, and stealthily made his way to the door which he opened to allow entry for Susan Atkins and Patricia Krenwinkel to enter, before instructing Kasabian to keep watch of the gate.

Being the youngest of the group that had been dispatched from Spahn Ranch by Charles Manson, Tex Watson who had been put in charge of taking care of business was unsure as to whether Linda Kasabian would have what it took to carry out their mission, therefore after sending her to keep watch of the main gate she made her way to where the group had pushed Parent's AMC Ambassador after he was murdered and waited.

Once inside Tex Watson, Susan Atkins and Patricia Krenwinkel went about creating hell, all as part of the plan by Charles Manson to start a race-war between whites and blacks.

Under the philosophy of 'Helter Skelter' – a name he stole from a song by the group The Beatles, Charles Manson had begun preaching to his followers that the minority black race would revolt against the superior whites and overthrow them from power.

However, now with the responsibility of power, and due to corruption, in-fighting and constant challenges for power the black race would not be able to handle the power and would look for survivors of the white race – which considering the number of hidden caves and hid-outs around Spahn Ranch that The Family had created – would mean that Manson would be called upon to unite the people and have all the power.

To speed things along with the race-war Manson had decided to have his Family Members to kill some high profile white folks and frame the uprising and ever growing Black Panther militia as the culprits.

Tex Watson was whispering to Susan Atkins in the main living area of the house, their whispering to each other however awoke a sleeping Wojciech Frykowski who was on the couch in the living room.

Watson kicked Frykowski in the head after the house guest asked him who he was and what he was doing there. Bending down to the injured man Watson proclaimed:

"I am the devil, and I'm here to do the devils business,"

Following Watson's directions Atkins found the houses three other occupants, with the help of Krenwinkel and forced them all into the living room of the house.

Once all of the houses occupants were in the living room Tex Watson began to tie, with rope he had brought with him, Sharon Tate and Jay Sebring together by their necks with the rope then slung over one of the supporting beams in the room.

Sebring voiced his concern over the rough treatment of eight-and-a-half month pregnant Sharon Tate. To shut him up Tex Watson shot Sebring.

Abigail Folger, heiress to the Folger Coffee Fortune, was taken back to her room momentarily where she retrieved her purse and gave the intruders the $70 that was inside, to save her life.

Watson turned his attention back to Sebring who continued to cry out in agony from the gunshot and would not comply with the commands to be quiet. Watson then stabbed Sebring seven times.

Frykowski was able to loosen his hands, which had previously been tied with a towel, and he began to struggle with Susan Atkins who had been entrusted with the job of guarding him by Tex Watson.

During the tussle between the two Susan Atkins began slashing at the legs of Wojciech Frykowski with a knife she had been using to threaten and intimidate him with as she guarded him.

Frykowski fought his way to, and out of, the front door and onto the porch where he looked to escape.

However, Tex Watson gave chase and the former school boy athlete quickly caught up with him and struck him over the head several times, stabbed him repeatedly and shot him twice.

In the process of the assault the right grip of the gun broke.

Still keeping guard of the front gate Linda Kasabian heard what she later described as "horrifying sounds" and ran from the driveway to the front door of the main house.

Seeing the gruesome scene that confronted her when she reached the front door Kasabian lied to Susan Atkins and yelled over the top of the screaming and crying that someone was coming.

But her warning was ignored by Tex Watson, Susan Atkins and Patricia Krenwinkel who continued with the mission they had been sent to do.

Abigail Folger had by this time escaped Krenwinkel and had run out to the pool area through a bedroom door, Patricia Krenwinkel gave chase and eventually caught up with Folger in the properties front lawn.

Krenwinkel began to stab the coffee heiress, before she was joined by Charles 'Tex' Watson and together they stabbed Abigail Folger 28-times.

Such was the degree of viciousness that police, who would be alerted to the crime by the maid the following morning, originally thought and described Abigail Folger as having been wearing a red dress – her dress was in fact white and was heavily stained with her own blood.

Wojciech Frykowski continued to fight for his life, and despite the injuries he had already suffered made his way to the lawn where Tex Watson caught up with him again and delivered a final flurry of stabbings killing the aspiring screenwriter with a total of 51 stab wounds.

Inside the house Sharon Tate was begging for her life, begging to Susan Atkins to let her live long enough to give birth to her unborn child.

The up and coming Hollywood starlet even offered herself up as a hostage, who would die in any way or fashion the murderous intruders wanted once she had given birth.

It was at this point that Charles Watson stabbed Tate 16-times killing her and her unborn child. In a book released after his incarceration Watson claims that as he was killing Tate she had cried out *"Mother... mother ..."* before taking her final breath.

With the occupants of the house now all dead, there was only one more task that had been bestowed upon them from Charles Manson – to do something '*witchy*' that would help get people talking about the murders.

Susan Atkins retrieved the towel that had previously been used to restrain Wojciech Frykowski and dipped it into the blood of Sharon Tate. Before writing on the front door of the property the word PIG.

The macabre scene was discovered on the morning of August 9th by Tate's housekeeper, Winifred Chapman, who had arrived at the Benedict Canyon estate leased by Sharon Tate and her husband Roman Polanski, to carry out her regular duties.

Police arrived on scene and took the only survivor at the address, the property's caretaker William Garretson, in for questioning. Garretson lived in the guest house that was located on the property, but a short distance from the main house, and not immediately visible. As the first suspect, Garretson was questioned and submitted to a polygraph test.

Garretson stated that Parent had visited him at approximately 11:30p.m. and left shortly thereafter. Garretson informed police that he was not involved in the murders and did not know anything that could help the investigation. Police accepted his explanation and he was released a short time later.

Inspector Harold Yarnell from the Los Angeles Police Department, and who oversaw the Tate Murder investigation, said at the time that his only suspect walked out of police headquarters *"There is not sufficient evidence to hold Garretson. There is no reason to suspect him."*

The news of the death of Sharon Tate, Jay Sebring, Abigail Folger, Wojciech Frykowski and Steven Parent shocked Hollywood with many of the stars at the time wondering whether this was some sort of attack on their profession.

Several possible motives were voiced, including a narcotics deal gone wrong, or fellow entertainers hiring a hitman due to missing out on roles either to Sharon Tate or in films directed by her husband Roman Polanski.

Police began to investigate all the leads that were available to them, however before their investigations could get into full swing they were swiftly called away with reports of another brutal homicide nearby.

It was the morning of August 10th, 1969, the usually peaceful Waverly Drive was disturbed by the sounds of approaching police vehicles rushing to the scene, the harrowing scream from 21-year-old Susan Struthers could be heard and marked a moment where the Los Feliz section of Los Angeles would never be the same again.

Officers jumped from their vehicles that had come to a screeching halt and ran towards the neat, tree-lined home sitting gently on a sloping hilltop at 3301 Waverly Drive.

As the first officers ran into the house, others who arrived minutes later comforted the 21-year-old daughter of Leno and Rosemary LaBianca.

Susan Struthers had arrived at her parents' property with her boyfriend Joe Dorgan after they failed to pick up the phone despite numerous attempts to call them.

The scene was grisly, disturbing and bloody – however police were quick to determine that the two bodies they had found inside were that of Leno and Rosemary LaBianca.

Leno LaBianca was born Pasquilino Antonio LaBianca in Los Angeles, California, on August 6, 1925. He took his first name, which was shortened to Lino, from his grandfather and his middle name from his father, an Italian tradition.

Both Lino's parents, Antonio and Corina LaBianca came to America in the beginning of the century.

Antonio had a growing grocery business with Gateway Ranch Markets and State Wholesale Grocery Company. The latter purchased food at wholesale prices and distributed it to a group of grocers.

Meanwhile Corina stayed at home taking care of Lino and his two older sisters Emma and Stella.

In High School Lino was an exceptional student, which led him to skip a grade. As a member of the Benjamin Franklin High School track team, Flash (his nickname) competed in both shot put and discus competitions.

People were constantly mispronouncing Lino's name, so he decided to change the spelling from "l" to "e".

Outside of school Leno worked for his father at Gateway Markets. In his free time, he frequented places like the Hollywood Roller dome, the Sycamore Drive-In and the Pasadena Civic Auditorium with his girlfriend Alice Skolfield.

According to Skolfield when interviewed after Leno's murder she said he was *"quiet, shy and equipped with a subtle humour,"* and *"had a great capacity for getting himself innocently into all kinds of trouble"*.

In 1949, Leno's father brought a home on Waverly Drive in the Los Feliz district of Los Angeles. This put Leno in another school and away from Alice. It wasn't too long before Leno forged his father's name on a change of address form and went back to Benjamin Franklin High School to be with his first love.

In the fall of 1942, Leno started working at State Wholesale as well as enrolling at Los Angeles City College, studying Business Administration.

After one semester at city college Leno transferred to the University of Southern California and went back to work at Gateway.

In November of 1943, Leno received his Army induction papers and was sent to For Macarthur in San Pedro California, and eventually went on to become a member of the 524th Military Police Battalion.

The following month he and Alice got engaged. They married in March of 1944 and lived for brief periods in Salinas, California and Gainesville, Texas.

In September, Leno was ordered off to Europe to serve in World War II and the couple was separated for 18 months while he was on duty in England, France, Holland and Germany.

During this period Alice lived with Leno's parents on Waverly Drive, eagerly waiting for him to come home as Leno was on the move in Europe.

He finally returned home in March of 1946 having risen to the rank of Technical Sergeant. Leno immediately joined the Army reserve where he took the rank of Sergeant First Class.

Back home, Leno's parents had his life planned out for him; he and Alice would live in the apartment behind the Waverly Drive house. As their family grew and they needed more space, they would move into the main house.

Alice desperately wanted her and Leno to have a home and a life of their own. Their marriage suffered as Leno tried hard not to hut his parents' feelings.

Unhappy with the marriage, Alice left. The couple talked briefly about divorce but after spending some time apart they reconciled and purchased a small home of their own in Alhambra.

Leno became a father in the spring of 1948 when Alice gave birth to Corina Jane LaBianca. Two years later Leno was elected to the Board of Directors and was named Vice President of both Gateway Markets and State Wholesale.

That December, Leno and Alice were blessed with their first son, Anthony Carl LaBianca.

In 1951, Leno and Alice purchased a bay front summer home on Newport Beach. They had use of the house for two weeks in June and rented it out the rest of the year.

In August Leno's father passed away. Leno became president of Gateway and State Wholesale and moved his family back into the property at Waverly Drive. Alice committed herself to getting her degree in Accounting, while Leno found himself buried in work from his new responsibilities.

Throughout the years, Leno and Alice began to grow apart, and while they still cared for each other they both wanted different things from life. In January of 1955 they agreed to separate, they both found separate apartments in Los Angeles and moved out of the Waverly Drive house.

In September of that year Leno became a father for the third time when Alice gave birth to Louise LaBianca.

State Wholesale was becoming more and more of a burden for Leno, he therefore decided to sell the business and focus his attention on the expansion of Gateway Markets.

Leno and Alice officially divorced, and he finally graduated from USC with Bachelors in Finance.

In 1959, Leno met Rosemary Struthers. The two fell in love and were married later that year in Las Vegas.

Leno had begun living out his life-long dream of breeding and racing thoroughbred horses.

He was tired of the grocery business and was looking for a way out of his responsibilities at Gateway.

Rosemary started her own business and was very successful. The two brought a house in Los Feliz previously owned by Walt Disney.

The houses needed a lot of work and turned out to be more trouble than it was worth.

In 1968, Leno sold the Disney house and brought the Waverly Drive house from his mother. Leno, Rosemary, and her son Frank moved in.

But only planned to stay there until Leno was officially finished at Gateway. In the summer of 1969 there were several break-ins at the Waverly Drive house.

Leno had finally come to an agreement with the other shareholders at Gateway that would allow him to get out of the business for good.

In August of 1969, Rosemary's son Frank spent a week vacationing with his friend Jim Saffie on Lake Isabella. Early in the week, Leno drove up to the lake and dropped off his boat for the boys to use.

On Saturday August 9th, both Leno and Rosemary drove up to Lake Isabella to pick up Frank and the boat. Frank was having such a good time, Leno and Rosemary decided he could stay another day and return to Los Angeles with the Saffie family.

At around nine that night Rosemary, Leno, and Rosemary's daughter Suzan left Lake Isabella with the speedboat and started heading back to Los Angeles.

Rosemary and Leno arrived at Waverly Drive at about 1.a.m. on Sunday morning after dropping off Suzan and stopping at a newsstand for a paper and racing form.

Leno was an avid gambler and spent a lot of time at the racetrack; at that time however, the only thing his gambling was winning him was a debt valued at $230 000.

Rosemary seemed quite disturbed about the news of the Tate murders, she retired to her bedroom while Leno fell asleep in the living room while reading the sports page.

It is believed that Rosemary LaBianca was born in Mexico on December 15th, 1929. Her parents, who were reported to be Americans, either abandoned her or died prematurely.

She grew up in an Arizona orphanage until the age of twelve, when a Californian family by the name of Harmon adopted her.

In the late 1940s, Rosemary met Frank Struthers while working as a carhop at the Brown Derby Drive-In in the Los Feliz district of Los Angeles.

The pair got married shortly thereafter. During her marriage to Frank Struthers, Rosemary gave birth to 2 children, Suzan, who was conceived out of an extra-marital affair in 1948, and Frank Jr. in 1955.

In 1958 Rosemary and Frank Struthers decided to get a divorce. A year later she met Leno LaBianca while working as a waitress at the Los Feliz Inn. The two fell in love, and one weekend rushed down to Las Vegas to get married.

Rosemary got along well with Leno's children. Suzan and Frank were about the same age as Leno's daughter Cory and son Anthony. Rosemary's sophisticated style and fashion sense was a big hit with Cory.

According to Leno's first wife Alice, Rosemary *"showed Cory new ways to wear her hair"* and *"spent time doing things with her that I didn't have time for."*

In 1968 Leno, Rosemary and Frank moved into Leno's childhood home on Waverly Drive. It was there, the following summer that a few odd occurrences frightened them.

Rosemary told a friend, *"someone is coming in our house while we're away. Things have been gone through and the dogs are outside the house when they should be inside."*

It wasn't the first time the house had been broken into; in August of 1943, while Leno was in his late teens, the house had been robbed while the family slept.

In May of 1969, Rosemary wrote to Leno's daughter Cory. *"We haven't had any more robberies, but every time I come home I expect to either find someone in the house or something missing. I think the police have stopped working on the case and we haven't heard anything from the insurance company."*

Earlier in the night six Family members, Leslie Van Houten, Steve "Clem" Grogan, and the four family members from the previous night drive out on Manson's order.

Displeased by the panic of the victims at Cielo Drive, Manson accompanied the six *"to show them how to do it."* After a few hours' ride, in which he considered a few murders and event attempted one of them, Manson gave Linda Kasabian directions that brought the group to 3301 Waverly Drive.

This was the home of supermarket executive Leno LaBianca and his wife, Rosemary, a dress shop co-owner. The house was next door to a house at which Manson and Family members had attended a party the previous year.

Shortly after falling asleep Leno LaBianca was awoken at gunpoint by Charles Manson and Tex Watson. Leno was assured by the intruders that he would not be hurt they were simply there to rob him.

Charlie removed a leather thong from his neck and had Tex use it to tie up Leno's hands. Leno was asked if there was anyone else in the house.

Leno told the two intruders that his wife was in the bedroom. Manson awoke Rosemary at gunpoint and allowed her to put a dress on over her nightgown before he led her into the living room where Tex Watson was finishing tying Leno's hands together with the leather thong.

Charlie and Tex reassured the couple that they wouldn't be hurt and were just being robbed. After collecting all the cash in the house Manson had Tex bring Rosemary back to her bedroom where he placed a pillowcase over her head and gagged her with a lamp cord.

He told her to stay quiet and remain in the room, which she did. Tex then returned to the living room, carrying a pillowcase to put it over Leno's head and then gagged his mouth with a lamp cord, Charlie left and within a few minutes Leslie Van Houten and Patricia Krenwinkel entered the residence where they were instructed by Tex to go to Rosemary's bedroom.

Tex began stabbing Leno with a bayonet. Leno screamed out *"stop stabbing me"*. The stabbing did stop, but only briefly as Tex was called into the bedroom by Van Houten and Krenwinkel who were having trouble with Rosemary after she had heard her husband scream out.

"what are you doing to my husband?" Rosemary yelled before she began flailing around the room still blinded by the pillowcase on her head.

The girls called out to Tex for help; Rosemary was swinging the lap still attached to the cord used to gag her. Tex lunged forward and stabbed her until she fell to the floor.

By the time the stabbing ended, Watson, Krenwinkel and Van Houten had stabbed Rosemary 41 times.

Leno was still alive when Tex made his way back to the living room where the stabbing resumed. After Tex was finished either he or Patricia Krenwinkel carved the word "WAR" into Leno's stomach.

Patricia Krenwinkel then stabbed him several times and left a carving fork protruding from his stomach and a steak knife from his throat.

The girls then wrote *"death to pigs"*, *"rise"* and *"healter skelter"* on the wall and refrigerator in Leno's blood.

The pair were forced to hitchhike their way back to Spahn Ranch as Charles Manson had directed Linda Kasabian to drive to the Venice home of an actor acquaintance of hers, another "piggy".

Depositing the other three Family members who had departed Spahn with him that evening at the man's apartment building, Manson then drove back to Spahn Ranch leaving them and the LaBianca killers to hitchhike home. Kasabian thwarted this murder by deliberately knocking on the wrong apartment door and waking a stranger.

On August 12th, 1969 the LAPD told the press it had ruled out any connection between the Tate and LaBianca homicides. Just four days later on August 16th the sheriff's office raided Spahn Ranch and arrested Manson and 25 others, as "suspects in a major auto theft ring" that had been stealing Volkswagen Beetles and converting them into dune buggies.

Manson laughed when he was informed what they were being arrested for, originally thinking the police had linked the family to the murders they had committed.

Weapons were seized during the raid on Spahn Ranch, but, because the warrant had been misdated, the group was released a few days later.

In a report at the end of August when virtually all leads had gone nowhere, the LaBianca detectives noted a possible connection between the bloody writings at the LaBianca house and "*the singing group the Beatles*" most recent album.

Following up on some leads, that had originally not looked promising, detectives investigating the LaBianca murders searched for crimes with similarities.

Talking to Kitty Lutesinger, who had been arrested with the members of the Manson Family, the detectives contacted members of a motorcycle gang Manson had previously tried to enlist as his bodyguards while the Family was at Spahn Ranch. While the game members were providing information that suggested a link between Manson and the murders, a dormitory mate of Susan Atkins had a story to share.

The dormitory mate of Susan Atkins informed LAPD of the Family's involvement in the crimes. Atkins was booked for the murder of Gary Hinman which took place on July 27th, 1969.

Incorrectly believing that Gary Hinman had considerable stocks and bonds and owned his property, Charles Manson had sent Bobby Beausoleil along with Mary Brunner and Susan Atkins to his home on July 25th to convince Gary to join the Family, which included turning over the assets Manson thought Hinman had inherited.

The three held the uncooperative Hinman hostage for two days, during which Manson showed up with a sword to slash his ear. After that, Beausoleil stabbed Hinman to death, ostensibly on Manson's instruction.

Before leaving the Topanga Canyon residence, Susan Atkins used Hinmans' blood to write "Political piggy" on the wall and to draw a panther paw – the Black Panther militia symbol.

It was after talking to Manson Family Member Kitty Lutesinger, who was the girlfriend of Bobby Beausoleil, that detectives were able to connect the Manson Family, and Charles Manson and Susan Atkins, to being involved in the murder of Gary Hinman.

On August 6th, 1969 Bobby Beausoleil was arrested after he had been caught driving Hinman's car, upon searching the murder weapon in the tire well.

Two days later, Manson told Family members at Spahn Ranch, *"Now is the time for Helter Skelter."*

Incarcerated for the murder of Gary Hinman at Sybil Brand Institute, a detention centre in Los Angeles, Susan Atkins begun talking to bunkmates Ronnie Howard and Virginia Graham, to whom she gave accounts of the events in which she had been involved in.

The story told to bunkmates were told to detectives and on December 1st, 1969, acting on the information from these sources, the LAPD announced for warrants for the arrest of Tex Watson, Patricia Krenwinkel, and Linda Kasabian in the Tate case; the suspects' involvement in the LaBianca murders was noted.

Before long physical evidence such as Krenwinkel's and Watson's fingerprints, which had been collected by the LAPD at Cielo Drive was augmented by evidence recovered by the public.

On September 1, 1969, the distinctive .22-caliber Hi Standard "Buntline Special" revolver Watson used on Parent, Sebring and Frykowski had been found and given to the police by 10-year-old Steven Weiss who lived near the Tate residence.

In mid-December when the Los Angeles Times published a crime account based on information Susan Atkins had given her attorney, Weiss' father made several phone calls which finally prompted the LAPD to locate the gun in its evidence file and connect it with the murders via ballistics tests.

Acting on that same newspaper account, a local ABC television crew quickly located and recovered the bloody clothing discarded by the Tate killers. The knives discarded en route from the Tate residence were never recovered, despite a search by some of the same crewmen and months later by LAPD.

A knife found behind the cushion of a chair in the Tate living room was apparently that of Susan Atkins, who lost her knife during the attack.

Tex Watson, Charles Manson, Patricia Krenwinkel and Susan Atkins were all convicted on all 27-charges they were arrested for.

They all received the Death Penalty during sentencing, however escaped execution when the California Supreme Court's People v. Anderson decision resulted in the invalidation of all death sentences imposed in California prior to 1972.

The sentences were commuted to Life in Prison

Charles 'Tex' Watson was found guilty of the murders of seven people; his seven counts were to be served concurrently. His minimum eligible parole date was November 26, 1976, but he has been denied parole 17 times since then.

He remains incarcerated at the Richard J. Donovan Correctional Facility in San Diego, California.

Susan Atkins was convicted for her participation in eight killings, including the Tate Murders. At the time of her death on September 24th, 2009 at the age of 61 she was California's longest-serving female inmate.

Linda Kasabian was offered immunity from prosecution for her role in the murders in exchange for turning state's evidence.

Patricia Krenwinkel overtook fellow Manson Family member Susan Atkins as the longest-incarcerated female inmate in the California penal system following Atkins' death in 2009.

She remains incarcerated at the California Institution for Women in Chino, California where as of her latest parole hearing on June 22, 2017 the 69-year-old has been denied fourteen times and will be eligible to have another parole suitability hearing in five years' time.

Charles Manson was convicted of first-degree murder and conspiracy to commit murder for the deaths of seven people, all of which were carried out at his instruction by members of his group.

Constables Kim Stephenson and Geoff Wyllie were the first to enter the gruesome scene that would shock even the most seasoned officers on the New Zealand Police Force.

"I was making the coffee and Kim wasn't feeling very well and thinking of going home again and then the call came over the radio," Constable Geoff Wyllie recounted at the 2009 retrial of David Bain.

"We had very little information to go on. Just go to 65 Every Street and the whole family is dead. We couldn't get any more information immediately," the Constable who at that time had been on the job for three-and-a-half-years said from the witness box while giving his evidence.

The two officers made their way up the path towards the front door to the house – once a handsome but gloomy property built around 1850 whose best days had well and truly passed by the time the Bains brought it 1974 and on this fateful morning was almost beyond repair – the pair saw the silhouette of a head and shoulders in one of the windows by the front door.

Remembering the Aramoana Killings taking place just 20km North-West from where they stood, on this cold wintery morning, just four years earlier, in which David Gray shot and killed thirteen people including police officer Stewart Guthrie, Constables Stephenson and Wyllie turned their torches off and stood still waiting to see what the silhouette would do.

From his position to the right of the front door Wyllie looked through the window, noticing that some of the long curtains were tattered allowing him to see small unobstructed snippets from inside the property.

"I could see a firearm on the floor and I could see a hand." Wyllie recalls.

Constables Kim Stephenson and Geoff Wyllie were joined on scene by Constable Les Andrews and Sergeant Murray Stapp, all arming themselves with their issued .38 police revolvers they once again approached the house and tried to get 22-year-old David Bain to open the door.

"I remember asking him to open the door and he said no. I asked him **'Where's your father?'** *Often it's the father in these matters and he just pointed across the hall."*

Constable Geoff Wyllie testified at the 2009 retrial of David Bain, claiming the exchange took place after cautiously approaching the window he and partner Kim Stephenson had seen the silhouette earlier – now identified as David Bain.

With the firearm accounted for Wyllie believed they were probably dealing with a murder-suicide however with Bain apparently too upset and in shock to move or talk the officers on scene needed to force entry to the property.

Despite not feeling the best Constable Kim Stephenson gave the front door three solid kicks, but the door didn't budge an inch.

Somewhat surprisingly considering that the house was so run down, and weathered, it looked as though one gust of strong wind would bring the entire structure crashing to the ground.

Sergeant Stapp used a piece of firewood from the stack on the veranda to break a pane in the door before cleaning the glass out of the frame using his revolver and unlocking the door from the inside.

Bursting through the front door the police officers found themselves tripping over knick-knacks that were sprawled throughout the property, the Bains had a reputation of being hoarders and in the light of day their homestead could easily be described as in squalor conditions.

David Bain was sitting on the floor, in the foetal positions at the end of the bed in his room, a room later described by police as the neatest of all the rooms inside the property.

Directly across the hallway another room where the body of Robin Bain, aged 58, lay on the ground a .22 rifle immediately to his side.

LOWER LEVEL

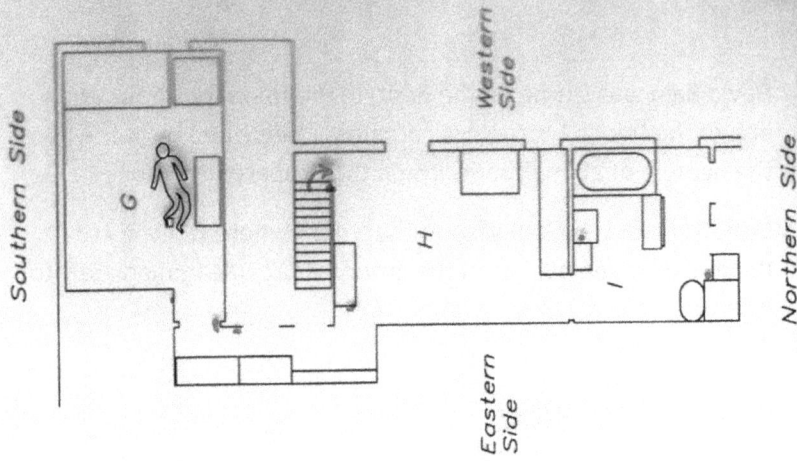

Southern Side

G

H

Western
Side

Eastern
Side

Northern Side

GROUND LEVEL

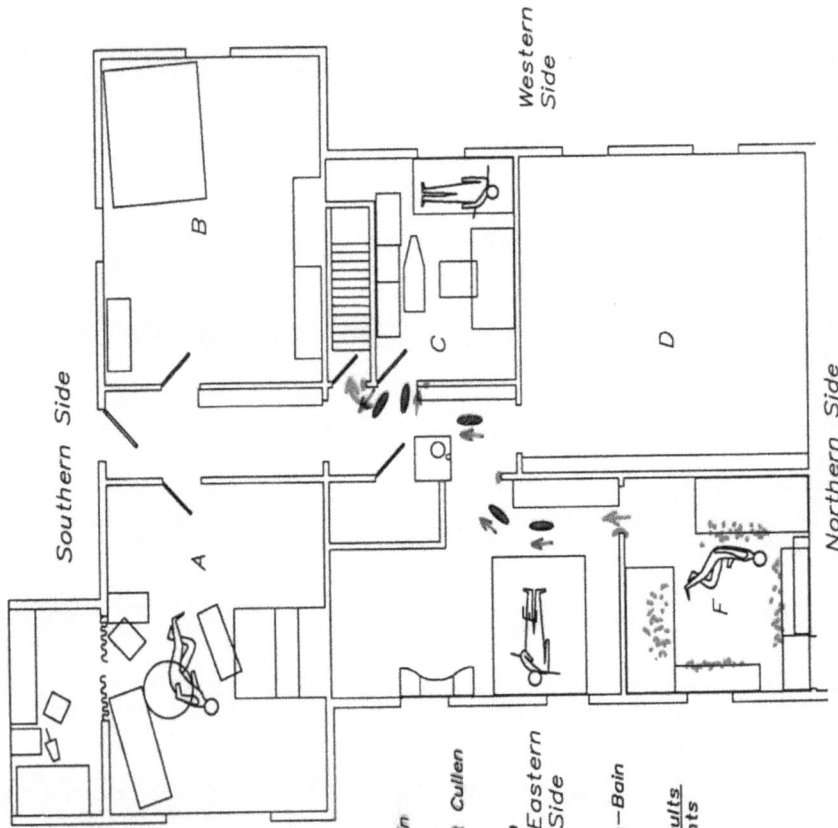

Southern Side

B

C

D

A

Western
Side

F

Northern Side

Room A
Mr Robin Bain

Room E
Mrs Margaret Cullen

Room F
Stephen Bain

Room C
Laniet Bain

Eastern
Side

Room G
Arawa Cullen-Bain

Luminol Results
Five footprints

Blood

SCALE

5 metres

WORKS
Consultancy Services

DUNEDIN

/POLICE

TITLE
65 EVERY STREET
ANDERSONS BAY
DUNEDIN

Constable Andrews stood at the door, and slowly raises his revolver to cover Constable Geoff Wyllie and Sergeant Murray Stapp as they venture down the cluttered hallway.

Constable Kim Stephenson asks David *"How many live in the house?"*

To which, in between sobbing and wailing, the 22-year-old David Bain replies *"There are six of us."*

Constable Stephenson leaves David Bain under the supervision of Constable Andrews and ventures to the room immediately across from where David was sitting, and where Constable Wyllie earlier saw the point-22 rifle and the hand through the window and finds the body of Robin Bain – the rifle laying on the ground at right angles to his body.

Robin is discovered fully clothed, with just one bullet wound near his left temple.

Constable Wyllie had only made it as far as the next bedroom on the left, where shining his torch to break up the early morning darkness he discovers the next body.

"There's one in here," he proclaims.

The body is that of Laniet Bain, aged 18, whose lying under a duvet cover on the bed which is positioned against the far wall of the room.

She has suffered three bullet wounds to the head, one through the top of her head and two located close to her left ear.

On the right of the hallway was another room with a curtain across the entrance in place of a door.

Sergeant Murray Stapp pushes the curtain off to one side with the barrel of his revolver.

And with faded light sees the body of a woman in the bed, under a thick duvet cover.

Sergeant Murray Stapp had discovered the body of Margaret Bain, aged 50, she has been shot once just above her left eye.

In the same room Sergeant Stapp sees another doorway and thinks it must lead to either a wardrobe or dressing room and doesn't investigate further.

Between David's room and the room in which Laniet's body lays dead there is a stairway leading to a lower level of the house.

Sergeant Stapp and Constable Wyllie cautiously make their way down the steps.

As the reach the bottom of the stairway they turn right, and find themselves in a dirty kitchen, whose benchtop is sprawled with dirty dishes.

With the adrenaline running through their veins Sergeant Stapp covers Constable Wyllie as he turns right again and disappears down a short narrow hallway which is lined by shelves, filled with bottled fruit and other preserves.

Wyllie comes face to face with another doorway which is covered by two curtains, a net curtain and a curtain made by metal rings.

"I pulled the curtain back and looked into that room," Wyllie told the court at the retrial of David Bain in 2009, *"And saw the body of another female on the floor in there,"*

"A couple steps down into that room and from where I was standing, she was sort off on bent back, like on her knees but bent back but looking straight at the doorway where I was standing."

The former Constable testified to the court when asked to describe how the body – that of Arawa, aged 19, was positioned when he discovered her.

"She had quite an obvious wound to her forehead."

Arawa had been shot once, the bullet entering the right side of her forehead, she is wearing a green jersey and pink pyjamas and a track of blood spots can be seen on her thighs.

As police continue to investigate the lower level of the property there was a sickening silence throughout the house, all that could be heard was David Bain from his bedroom wailing and screaming.

Standing at the bottom of the stairs Constable Wyllie calls out to his colleagues that they have found four bodies.

Constable Kim Stephenson calls back to inform his partner that there should be six in the house including David.

Constable Wyllie goes to recheck the downstairs area, while Sergeant Stapp heads back into the room where he discovered the body of Margaret Bain to investigate further.

Behind the curtain, in which Sergeant Stapp assumed earlier was a wardrobe, he finds another bedroom and immediately discovers the body of 14-year-old Stephen Bain lying on the floor.

Stapp immediately knew that Stephen was dead and retreated from the room.

The youngest Bain sibling has three bullet wounds, one in the top of his head, and the other bullet has gone through the palm of his left hand and into his head.

Due to the amount of blood in the room, and the wound to Stephen's hand Police are immediately under the belief that there had been a struggle and that the fourteen-year-old had fought for his life against the person or persons who had effectively wiped out an entire family.

It was quickly becoming apparent to everyone at the scene that there were only two people who could have been responsible for the carnage.

Father Robin Bain, reports flooding into the police in the days following the shootings suggested that Robin had been cast out of the family, his marriage had deteriorated to the point that Robin spent the weeknights in the school house at the Taieri Beach School of which he was the Principal at, before returning to the property and staying in a caravan on the weekends.

Other Principals who regularly interacted with Robin told police they had feared he had deteriorated mentally and physically.

Not getting interviews for other roles that he had applied for, and to many it seemed that he had lost his passion for teaching, and no longer being motivated.

Although he was proud and very fond of all his children it was suggested that at the time of the shootings he had hit rock-bottom and was struggling.

It was said that Robin was frustrated and down about his career and at wits end over his marriage breakdown with Margaret.

Many suggested that he seemed to become more frail as the worry got to him and he became overwhelmed with depression.

The other possible culprit in the house was the only member of the family who remained alive 22-year old David Bain.

David had recently begun a part time course at the University of Otago studying in classics and music papers.

His studies gave him the freedom to stay on the dole, while also giving him the time to help his mother in the gardens as they worked on their plans to replace the eroding Every Street property with a new house.

However, investigations by police following the deaths revealed that David hated his father.

Since the demise of the marriage between Robin and Margaret, in which Robin had effectively moved into the school house at Taieri Beach School, by all reports it was David who had become the head of the house.

All responsibilities had fallen onto his shoulders and he was reported to be excited about the new house in which both he and Margaret were deeming 'The Sanctuary' – a seven-bedroom property doubling as a wellness centre.

Tensions between David and his father Robin however continued to rise on the weekends when Robin, desperate to save his marriage, would attempt to control the family on the weekend visits in which he returned home to stay in the caravan in the backyard of the property.

David reportedly told a friend in the week before the murder that he felt as though "*he didn't have any friends,*" and was too afraid to develop close friends as "*Anybody I have ever loved, I have hurt.*"

It could be argued that one of the most chilling statements to friends come from the young man prior to the shocking murders of his family came just days before the bodies were discovered when having a conversation in a friend's apartment he stated "*Tensions are so high. I think something bad is going to happen.*"

And for police, and an entire country, the mystery began – who killed the members of the Bain family?

What facts are widely accepted is on Friday, just days before the murders, Margaret spent the day at home, cleaning and getting the house ready.

A friend dropped by to lend her a VHS tape of one of David's recent performances in a community group production.

During this visit which lasted approximately half an hour the friend reports that Margaret was excited as it was the first time in a long time the entire family were all going to be together.

In addition to Arawa, Stephen and David her other daughter Laniet was also going to be at home for the first time in many months.

Laniet had left home in 1993, unable to cope with the growing tensions in the property as the marriage between Robin and Margaret continued to disintegrate.

She had rented a room in a boarding house in Russell Street where she started working as a freelance escort. Despite her best efforts in concealing the lifestyle to everyone it was obvious to how she was earning her money.

Arawa was in her second year at teachers' college and was completing university papers. She had a comfortable job as a server at the Museum Café as well as earning additional cash by babysitting.

Murder Suspect Robin Bain had spent Friday morning on the phone in relation to handicapped students to which he required additional funds to help, but as had become the usual, the paperwork was not completed.

Robin had claimed that he would get it fixed up over the weekend and re-submit the paperwork on Monday morning.

However, throughout the duration of the week leading up to the murders he had been calling around attempting to find a fill-in for him the following week.

David had completed some studies in the morning and arrived home to work on the garden with his mother in the afternoon.

By all reports that Friday evening the family had Fish and Chips for dinner with Margaret using the microwave to heat up the fish while David and Arawa went to the local takeaway shop to purchase the hot chips.

After dinner the family settled down to watch a nature documentary that David had borrowed off one of his friends, however Robin and Margaret then decided to change the film to a thriller.

On the day of the murders David claims he awoke and got dressed ready to execute his paper route.

For some reason, which he couldn't explained when questioned by police, he admitted he left early and to assist in his efforts to get fitter ran to complete the route.

He arrived home, took his now sweaty clothes off putting them into the washing machine before noticing that the light was on in his mother's room.

Upon entering the room, he found her body, scared and afraid he ran to the lounge room where his dad normally conducted his morning prayers only to find the body of his 58-year-old father.

This, David claims, is when he called the police.

While all signs pointed towards a Murder-Suicide carried out by Robin there were some aspects of the crime scene that didn't add up.

In the days following the murders the Otago Daily Times carried increasing coverage of the killings, while David, who at this point was staying with his uncle and aunty nearby, began the tough task of preparing for the funerals of his family.

Family members recalled at the retrial in 2009 that David was quite controlling over the funeral arrangements, having a special song picked out for each member of the family, and deciding that his mother and father would be cremated, while his two sisters and one brother would be buried.

"If a suggestion was made, that wasn't his, he would just shut it down or effectively switch off," one family member recounted.

Family and friends rallied around David, his close friend at the time telling of one conversation they had in the days immediately after the murders in which David reportedly said: *"I don't know what to say to the police to make them believe I didn't do it."*

Suspicion was increasing at Otago's CIB, and while Detectives on the case were determined to tread carefully with the knowledge that they were dealing with someone who had just lost his entire family and that rushing their process could have dire effects.

On the Friday, just four days following the murders, David was driven to CIB by his uncle Bob where three detectives were awaiting them as they exited the lift.

Detective Senior Sergeant Jim Doyle took Bob away for a cup of coffee while Detective Sergeant Croudis and Detective Neil

Lowden took David into an interview room for his fourth interview in as many days.

After being informed of his rights the interview officially commenced at 10:43 am.

Q. Your fingerprints have been found in blood on your firearm, why are they there?

A. I don't know.

Q. When you say I don't know, do you mean that you didn't touch the firearm, you didn't have blood on your hands or the forensic evidence is false?

A. I didn't touch the firearm to my knowledge. I didn't have blood on my hands as I'd washed them.

Q. Do you accept the forensic evidence I've outlined?

A. Yes.

Q. When we discussed that question earlier you stated you could not account for between 15-20 minutes. Is that an explanation for what happened to your family that morning?

A. No.

Q. What is it?

A. It's a question of what happened to me. After I saw my Father I remember seeing my family being pulled away by black hands.

Q. There is a blood stained fingerprint on the washing machine. How did that get there?

A. I don't know.

Q. Are you saying you didn't make it?

A. I can't say that because if it is my fingerprint then it is my hand that has put it there.

Q. There are indications of blood from clothing that appears to have been pushed into the washing machine. Can you tell me why blood-stained clothing has been washed?

A. No.

Q. Do you accept you washed clothes on Monday morning?

A. Yes.

Q. And in those clothes was at least one pair of socks belonging to you?

A. Yes.

Q. A sweatshirt belonging to you?

A. Yes.

Q. A dark jersey belonging to Arawa?

A. Yes.

Q. When the police located you at the house, you were wearing a white T-shirt with a Queen's Baton Relay emblem?

A. Yes.

Q. On the back of that shirt we have observed blood, how did that get there?

A. I don't know.

Q. If your previous statements to Detective Sergeant Dunne are truthful, then there should be no reason for that blood to be on your shirt?

A. No.

Q. When you were located by the police you were wearing white socks. We have located blood on the sole of the sock. How did that get there?

A. I don't know.

Q. Again, if your statement to Detective Sergeant Dunne is truthful there is no reason for you to have blood stained clothing.

A. Unless I stood in some blood.

Q. Where might you have stood in blood?

A. I don't know.

Q. We have located a spot of blood on the black rugby shorts you were wearing. Explain to me how that got there.

A. I can't.

Q. There is blood on the porcelain hand basin in the bathroom, how did that get there?

A. I don't know.

Q. Did you put it there?

A. No.

Q. There's blood on a large towel hanging in the bathroom, a considerable amount of blood. How did that get there David?

A. I don't know.

Q. We found blood on the door surround in Stephen's room. It was a small amount compared with the amount found inside Stephen's room. There had been a violent struggle in Stephen's room. Stephen had fought for his life. Can you tell me how that blood got there?

A. No.

Q. David, do you own any gloves?

A. Purple woollen gloves, fingerless gloves, and I've recently bought new white dress gloves for a ball at Lanarch Castle.

Q. Is that all?

A. Yes.

Q. Where are those gloves?

A. The purple ones should be in the top drawer of the wardrobe in my room, the green gloves are on the chair in my room. The white gloves are with my dress scarf in the same drawer as the purple gloves.

Q. Do you keep your dress clothes separate?

A. Not at all.

Q. The white gloves, do they have a button or gap?

A. No, they're plain.

Q. What are they made of?

A. Elasticated some sort, I don't know.

Q. Did anyone else in the house have dress gloves?

A. My Father.

Q. Where would those be?

A. In the caravan, I don't know where.

Q. You're certain he keeps his formal gear in the caravan?

A. Yes.

Q. In Stephen's room a pair of white formal type gloves were located. These were heavily bloodstained. Do you know anything about these?

A. No.

A. [David]. Can I have a solicitor present?

Q. Who do you want?

A. I don't know.

The time as 11:20am when David Bain asked for a solicitor, and through his uncle Bob Clark, Mr. Michael Guest arrived to represent the young man.

On the advice of Mr Guest, David Bain refused to answer any additional questions he also refused a request from police for a medical examination after Mr Guest flat out rejected attempts by the doctors to examine his client.

At 1:46pm that Friday afternoon Detectives formally charged David Bain with the murders of Robin, Margaret, Arawa, Laniet and Stephen.

After a brief court appearance, he was remanded in custody.

Prosecution Lawyers believed they had a strong case, and many questions relating to the murders remained unanswered.

While legal experts declared that the case was circumstantial, Defence attorneys were just as confident their client would be found innocent.

At approximately 9:30am on the morning of the murders David Bain asked a police officer tending to him, while the others on scene were exploring the house finding the bodies of the Bain family, for his glasses.

Constable van Turnhout saw a pair of glasses sitting on a chair and picked them up to hand them to David before realizing he shouldn't be touching them as they were part of a crime scene.

The glasses frame was damaged, and no lenses were in the frame, one lens remained on the chair that Constable van Turnhout had picked the frame up from, the other lens had been found in the room where the body of fourteen-year-old Stephen Bain was discovered.

It later transpired that the glasses belonged to Margaret Bain, they were an older pair that David used on an irregular basis when his were not available.

A week prior to the murders David had broken his glasses when he tripped in the garden when exiting his singing teachers' property with the glasses sent away for repair.

David later claimed that he only used the glasses when watching television or when he needed to attend lectures and his were unavailable.

Further adding to the mystery surrounding the glasses was the police's own crime scene photos in which it is claimed the lens found in Stephen's room was clearly seen in the photographs at the toe of an ice-skate.

However, when it these lens' were to be retrieved three days after the murders the lens was found under the ice-skate, raising concerns of contamination.

Mr Wright, the Crown Solicitor put the use and the ownership of the glasses squarely to David Bain in cross-examination as follows.

Q. The pair of glasses which you have produced to the court have a saxon frame?
A. Yes.

Q. You say they are not yours, but they are an older pair of your Mother's?
A. That's right.

Q. The ophthalmologist, Mr Sanderson, from the hospital was of the opinion that they were an earlier prescription of your existing optometry prescription?
A. That is incorrect. One of these lenses I would not be able to see out clearly to give me full vision.

Q. The ophthalmologist was of the opinion that the prescription of the two lenses that fitted the frame are similar to the prescription prescribed for you in October 1992. Do you recollect him giving that evidence?
A. I do, that is only in one lens though, not the other.

Q. Were those glasses of assistance to you?
A. Yes, for watching TV and for going to lectures, but I couldn't use them for extended periods.

Q. Did you have lectures on Friday 17 June?
A. As far as I can remember, yes, I did.

Q. Did you wear glasses at that lecture?
A. No, no. I had forgotten about those glasses here, the ones exhibited, because I only used them rarely and hadn't thought of getting them for classes.

Q. You have referred in your evidence to watching a video on TV over the weekend?
A. That is correct, yes.

Q. Did you use the glasses for that purpose?
A. No, I hadn't thought of using them.

Q. Where were these glasses kept to your knowledge?
A. In Mum's room. In one of her drawers, I suppose. I don't know exactly where.

Q. Were you aware the spectacle frames were in your room on the morning of 20 June?
A. No, I wasn't.

Q. Were you aware that the spectacle frames have apparently been damaged?
A. I am aware now of that, yes.

Q. Would the glasses have been any use to you, the frames, without the lenses in them?
A. I wouldn't have seen a reason for wearing them.

Q. Were the glasses in your room, the frame and the lens, in your room on the Sunday night?
A. No.

Q. Can you account for their presence as found in your room by the police on the Monday morning?
A. No, I cannot account for that.

Another crucial point in the prosecution of David Bain was the traces of blood police found leading from Stephen's room, using luminol – which reacts to blood, which at times is not visible to the naked eye, which luminates under black light.

When luminol was sprayed throughout the house at 65 Every Street in Dunedin five clear sock prints could be seen leading from Stephen's bedroom, through the bedroom of mother Margaret's down the hallway and to the top of the staircase leading downstairs.

The best two prints measured in at 280mm, and all were from the right foot.

Mr Peter Hentschel, the ESR Specialists that was brought in on the case referred to one of the prints that measured in at 280mm was as close to a full print as he has seen in a crime scene.

Detective Sergeant Milton Weir, who was assisting Hentschel prior to the first trial of David Bain in 1995 said that one of the prints looked as a print would if someone was walking through sand on a beach.

Several tests were undertaken by Kevan Walsh, a scientist employed by the ESR in Auckland relating to the length of the bloodied sock prints. There were several difficulties associated with this determination. Two are as follows.

[1] Because this type of print is visualised as a glow in the dark a direct measurement will have some inaccuracy.

[2] The print size will depend on the extent of staining on the sole.

Mr Walsh used his own foot for the tests. His foot is 298 mm in length. The result from those tests showed that a shorter print is made when standing rather than when walking.

The length of the prints made when walking never measured less than 280 mm and were mostly between 290 mm and 300 mm. From these experiments it could be concluded that a walking person with a 300 mm foot, which is the length of David Bain's foot, making sock prints with the sock completely bloodied, would be expected to make a print greater than 280 mm.

However, Kevan Walsh believed a print of 280 mm could be made. An examination was also completed of the socks of David Bain.

This test showed that the maximum length of the blood staining that would be printed by a person wearing the sock who had a 300 mm foot would be about 288 mm.

Depending on the position of the sock the length of blood staining could be as short as about 271 mm.

Further tests were done by Kevan Walsh in 2008.

Wearing a sock, he immersed his right foot in a tray of cow or pig's blood.

The length of the prints he made were never less than 280 mm and mostly between 290 mm and 300 mm.

He also did tests while standing and found a luminol visualised sock print measured between 269 mm and 287 mm with an average of 279 mm.

Mr Walsh also had a student with the same size foot as Robin Bain conduct tests. The average length of his luminol visualised walking print was 282 mm and the variance was from 273 to 292 mm.

No standing test was carried out.

Which effectively means that either of the main suspects in the case, both David and Robin Bane could have been responsible for the sock prints discovered under the luminol test.

However, it would be neglectful if we didn't discuss the biggest issue of the overall crime – that being the Bain family computer.

On it police found a note typed *"sorry, you are the only one that deserved to stay."*

The computer has been one of the most contentious points of the overall Bain Family Murders with experts arguing on everything from the time the computer was turned on, to who could have possibly typed the note.

The first computer expert brought in to examine the computer stated that the computer was turned on at 6:44am, however, after it was revealed that he was working on a watch that was two minutes fast this time was adjusted to 6:42am.

Another computer expert from the Police Electronic Crime Laboratory was commissioned to report on the time the computer was turned on.

His analysis employed more sophisticated technology than that which was available to the first computer expert. His analysis revealed a few previously unidentified issues in relation to the first computer experts' calculations.

These issues included time lags in the computer clock's mechanisms that the first expert was unaware of. According to his calculations the computer was turned on between 6.39.49 a.m. and 6.49.11 a.m.

No-one has been able to determine who turned the computer on, by David Bains own admission he should have been walking through the front door of the house at approximately 6:44 a.m.

While Robin Bain's alarm clock was set for 6:30 a.m. which meant that he could have easily made his way from the caravan in the backyard to the house by 6:35 a.m. to turn on the computer.

Experts also debate on who typed the message that sat flickering on the screen as Crime Scene Investigators scoured the house.

It is widely accepted though that had it been Robin Bain, who had a long career as a teacher and in later years a principal, he would have probably have written 'deserves' instead of the incorrect grammar of 'deserved'.

In addition, Robin wrote weekly letters to his mother, and brothers. It seems that it would have taken more time to start the computer and type the message in than it would've to write a note saying the same thing.

By writing a note Robin would have also immediately exonerated the one person who 'deserved' to stay.

With the trial already taking twists and turns, and a whole country divided with their beliefs that this 22-year-old student either killed his family, or for one reason or another was spared, it was several chilling testimonies and statements made to the police that threw an even bigger cloud over the entire ordeal.

In the month prior to the killings Laniet grew increasingly upset, she stated to close friends and neighbours that she was trying to get out of the escort business.

She stated that she found herself caught in a web as her pimp was threatening to expose her lifestyle to her parents, this added to Laniet's fear of going near the house, and especially her father.

She had confided in a neighbour *"He was doing things that were inappropriate to her,"* and claimed, *"Robin was touching her in ways he shouldn't be."*

While she didn't come out and say incest was happening neighbours and close friends state it was easy to figure out what she was talking about.

At David's retrial in 2009 Dean Cottell – who was rumoured to be Laniet's pimp – stated that he had seen Laniet on Friday afternoon and she had told him that her father *'was having sex with her'*.

He went on to further claim that Laniet was heading to her parents' house that weekend to tell them everything and get an opportunity for a fresh and clean start to life.

Meanwhile, friends of Arawa stated that they felt uneasy visiting the 18-year-old at the Every Street property. They claimed in statements to the police that it appears the teenager was always looking over her shoulder and avoided conversations out of fear she would be over heard.

One friend went as far as to say that Arawa had "*Things she couldn't tell anyone about. Some sort of family secret.*"

The family was disjointed, Robin was on the outside looking in according to friends and family. Margaret, David, Arawa and Stephen didn't want Robin around.

While Laniet was very supportive of Robin.

In May 1995 David Cullen Bain was convicted on all five counts of murder and was sentenced by the presiding Judge to the mandatory Life in Prison with a non-parole period of sixteen-years.

However, in 2007, twelve-years after first being sentenced, Bain's legal team – with the support of former All Black Joe Karam successfully appealed to the Privy Council, who declared there had been a '*substantial miscarriage of justice*'.

David Bain was released on bail in May 2007 where a retrial took place in 2009 which resulted with his acquittal on all charges.

Speculation about the case continued long after Bain was acquitted, including whether he should receive compensation for the years he spent in prison.

Canadian jurist Ian Binnie was appointed in November 2011 to review the circumstances and advise the government on whether compensation should be paid.

Binnie concluded that the Dunedin police made 'egregious errors' and that the 'extraordinary circumstances' in the case justified the payment of compensation.

This report was rejected by the Minister of Justice, on advice from **High Court Judge** Robert Fisher

In March 2015, the government appointed **Ian Callinan**, a retired justice of the **High Court of Australia**, to conduct a second review of Bain's compensation claim.

Ian Callinan's report, in which he concluded that Bain was not innocent on the balance of probabilities, was delivered to the Minister of Justice on the 26th of January 2016.

The Minister announced that no compensation would be paid, but that Bain would be given an **ex-gratia** payment of $925,000 if he agreed to stop all further legal action.

Bain accepted the ex-gratia payment and put a stop to all legal action he was perusing through the courts, David Bain has since married girlfriend Liz Davies, and legally changed his name through deed poll to William Davies – taking his wives surname.

On 3rd December 2014 they welcomed a baby boy into the world, and it was reported in early 2017 that the stigma surrounding ex-criminals has followed Bain preventing him from being able to find work to support his family and he was therefore moving to an undisclosed location in Australia.

KATHERINE KNIGHT
THE CANNIBAL OF ABERDEEN

It has been described as one of the most heinous crimes in Australian history, a crime that has seen the name Katherine Knight forge a way into the countries folklore – along the same lines as Ivan Milat, Martin Bryant and Bushranger Ned Kelly.

A crime that saw Knight become Australia's First Female Killer to be sentenced to Life in Prison and her file stamped "**NEVER TO BE RELEASED**."

Katherine Mary Knight was born on October 24th, 1955, as a twin to parents Ken Knight (father) and Barbara Roughan (mother) in Tenterfield, New South Wales – about three hours from Byron Bay.

She had been born and raised in an unconventional and dysfunctional family environment. Her mother – Barbara Roughan had been married to Jack Roughan with the pair residing in the small New South Wales town of Aberdeen where they together had four boys.

However, Barbara began an adulterous relationship with Ken Knight, a friend and co-worker of Jack Roughan.

Both the Roughan and Knight families were well-known in the conservative rural town and the affair was a major scandal and much the talking point amongst the housewives over coffee, or the husbands at the local pub over a cold beer at the end of the day.

Barbara and her lover Ken were forced to leave Aberdeen and moved to Moree, New South Wales located approximately three hours from Tamworth, the country music capital of Australia.

In addition to the four children from her previous relationship with Jack Roughan, none of whom moved with Barbara and Ken Knight to Moree, the pair had another four children which consisted of two boys and the twin girls Katherine and Joy.

When Katherine was just four years old her mother's husband Jack Roughan died, and the two boys from their marriage that had remained living with him soon moved in with Barbara and Ken.

As the children grew up it became more obvious to those on the outside to see that things were quite different in the Knight household.

The tempers of the children would see their moods change more often than the wind direction, sometimes at the drop of the hat the children would reportedly go from angelic creatures to something that some claim is best described as spawn from demonic origin.

Knight's father Ken was an alcoholic who openly used violence and intimidation to rape her mother up to ten times a day.

In turn Barbara would often tell her twin daughters intimate details of her sordid sex life.

Often discussing how much she hated sex and men, even later in life telling Katherine to *"put up with it and stop complaining"* when she complained about one of her lovers who wanted her to take part in a sex act that she did not want to perform.

Katherine Knight later claimed that she was regularly sexually assaulted by members of her own family (although not her father) which continued until she was around the age of eleven, a claim members of her family would later confirm did happen.

In 1969 the only person, apart from her twin sister Joy, that Katherine was close to – her Uncle Oscar Knight – a champion horseman committed suicide an act that devastated her.

That same year the family moved back to Aberdeen where Katherine began to attend Muswellbrook High School where she was considered as a loner, however, classmates remember her as a bully who stood over smaller children.

At least one boy at school was assaulted by Katherine Knight with a weapon, while a teacher was also injured by the out of control teenager.

Katherine Knight had claimed that the teacher had used excessive discipline, the teacher was later cleared of any inappropriate behaviour after it was found that they had acted in self-defence against the teenager during one of her out of control tantrums.

Such was the nature of the Knight children and their dramatic mood swings that when not in rage Katherine was a model student who often earned awards for her behaviour.

At the age of fifteen Katherine Knight left school, unable to read or write, she gained employment as a cutter at a local factory before leaving the employment just twelve months later to take up what she would describe as her dream job – cutting up offal at the local abattoir where she was quickly promoted to boning and given her own set of knives.

These knives would become Katherine's most prized possession and when not at work she would hang these knives above her bed citing that they *would always be handy if I needed them*", a habit she continued at every property she resided in until her incarceration.

Despite always showing her anger throughout her life, with incidents drastically developing into more violent encounters following her first marriage, Katherine Knight was never put into the prison system until she murdered her last boyfriend.

In 1974, Katherine Mary Knight, married first husband David Kellett however, her violent side didn't take long to come out when on their wedding night Katherine attempted to strangle her new husband because he fell asleep after having sexual intercourse just three times.

"You better watch this one or she'll fucking kill you. Stir her up the wrong way or do the wrong thing and you're fucked, don't ever think of playing up on her, she'll fuckin' kill you."

Were words of wisdom given to Kellett by Katherine Knights own mother, Barbara, on the day of their wedding, and hauntingly that evening David Kellett had seen a violent outburst, that he had seen many times previously in his relationship with Katherine, that made the ominous statement stick in his mind.

It wasn't long into their marriage when the first serious incident happened between the pair that made David Kellett fearful for his life.

After competing in a darts competition at the local pub, David had made it to the competitions finals and therefore was late home compared to the normal time he usually walked in the door.

Stepping foot in the house Knight struck David Kellett in the back of the head with a frying pan.

In fear for his life Kellett fled before collapsing in a neighbours house who called for an ambulance.

In the wake of being rushed to the hospital it was discovered that David Kellett had suffered from a badly fractured skill. Local police wanted to charge Katherine Knight, who by now was on her best behaviour and convinced Kellett not to pursue charges against her.

Over two turbulent years David Kellett put up with Katherines constant abuse before he fled town with another woman leaving Katherine abandoned with her new born child Melissa Ann.

Katherine fell deep into depression, and in next to no time she was seen pushing her new baby in a pram down the main street, violently throwing the pram from side to side.

Katherine Knight was admitted into St Elmo's Hospital, in Tamworth, for treatment from postnatal depression and spent several weeks receiving treatment and recovering.

With Melissa Ann just two months old Knight was witnessed placing her on a railway line shortly before the train was due, a local, known as "Old Ted", was foraging near the railway line and saw the baby being left, he ran and rescued Melissa, by all accounts only minutes before the train passed through.

Katherine Knight then stole an axe and went into town where she threatened to kill several people.

Katherine Knight was arrested, and again taken to St Elmo's Hospital but apparently recovered and signed herself out the following day.

While many had hoped this would be the wakeup call Katherine needed it took just two days for them to realize she was the same 'Kathy' they had grown to know and fear.

Katherine slashed the face of a woman with one of her knives and demanded that the woman drive her to Queensland to find her estranged husband, David Kellett.

The terrified woman was able to escape after they stopped at a service station for gas and the hostage was able to raise the alarm, by the time police responded Knight had taken a little boy hostage and was threatening him with a knife.

She was soon disarmed by police who attacked her with brooms and upon being taken into custody Katherine Knight was admitted to the Morisset Psychiatric Hospital.

Knight admitted during her time in the Morisset Psychiatric Hospital that she had intended to kill the mechanic at the service station because he had once repaired Kellett's car, which had allowed him to flee to Queensland with his new lover.

Katherine Knight went on to admit that her plan once arriving in Queensland was to kill both her husband, David Kellett, and his mother, who she claimed had constantly interfered in the marriage.

When police informed Kellett of what had transpired he left his girlfriend and along with his mother moved to Aberdeen to support Katherine, realising that the mentally unstable Knight would not stop hunting him while they were apart.

Knight was released from the Morisset Psychiatric Hospital on 9th August 1976, into the care of her mother-in-law and along with Kellett they moved to Woodridge, a suburb of Brisbane, where she had no trouble finding employment at the Dinmore meatworks in nearby Ipswich.

On 6th March 1980 Katherine and David had a second daughter Natasha Maree.

In 1984 Katherine Knight left David and moved in, first with her parents in Aberdeen, then to a rented house in nearby Muswellbrook.

Although she returned to work at the abattoir, she injured her back the following year and went on a disability pension.

No longer needing to rent accommodation close to her work the government gave her a Housing Commission property in Aberdeen.

Knight met 38-year-old miner David Saunders in 1986, and after a few months of dating he moved into her housing commission property with her and her two daughters, however kept his old apartment in Scone.

Katherine Knight soon became jealous regarding what he did when she was not around and would often throw him out, where he would move back to his apartment in Scone, where Knight would invariably follow and beg him to return.

In May 1987 Katherine cut the throat of David's' two-month-old dingo pup in front of him for no reason than showing what would happen to him if he had an affair or left her, before she went on to knock him unconscious with a frying pan.

In June 1988 Katherine Knight gave birth to her third daughter Sarah, which prompted Saunders to put a deposit on a house, which Knight paid off when her workers' compensation settlement came through in 1989.

Katherine took it upon herself to decorate the house which consisted of animal skins, skulls, horns, rusty animal traps, leather jackets, old boots, machetes, rakes and pitchforks throughout – no space, including the ceilings, were left uncovered.

Soon after the pair had a massive argument where Knight hit Saunders in the face with an iron before stabbing him in the stomach with a pair of scissors.

David moved back to Scone, but when he returned home found that she had cut up all his clothes.

Taking Long Service Leave from his employment Saunders went into hiding, where Katherine Knight tried desperately to find him, but no one admitted to knowing where he was.

Several months had passed and Saunders returned to the area to see his daughter Sarah only to find that Knight had gone to the police and told them that she was afraid of him.

They had issued her with an Apprehended Violence Order (AVO) against him.

In 1990 Katherine Knight became involved with 43-year-old former abattoir co-worker, John Chillingworth, and in 1991 gave birth to a boy the pair named Eric.

Their relationship lasted three years before Knight left him for a man she had been having an affair with for some time, John Price.

John "Pricey" Price was the father of three children when he and Knight had begun their affair.

Reputedly a "terrific bloke" liked by everyone who knew him, his own marriage had ended in 1988.

While his younger two-year-old daughter had remained with his former wife, the two older children lived with him.

'Pricey' was aware of Knight's violent reputation and in 1995 she moved into his house. Pricey's children liked her, and he was making a lot of money working in the local mines, apart from a few violent arguments, everyone who knew the couple suggested that *"life was a bunch of roses"*.

Things began to turn sour for the pair in 1998 when the couple had a fight over Price's refusal to marry her and in retaliation Knight videotaped items he had stolen from work and sent the tape to his boss.

Although the items were out of date medical kits that he had scavenged from the company rubbish tip, Price was fired from the job he had held for 17 years.

That same day he kicked her out and she returned to her own home while news of what she had done spread through the gossip-vine throughout town.

A few months later Price restarted his relationship with Knight, although he now refused to allow her to move in with him. The fighting between the pair became even more frequent and most of his friends would no longer have anything to do with him while he remained in the relationship citing that she brought out the *'worst in him'*.

A series of assaults, which culminated with Knight stabbing Price in the chest, was the final straw for the much-loved larrikin.

On 29th February 2000 on his way to work he stopped in at Scone Magistrate's Court and took out a restraining order to keep Katherine away from both he and his children.

Worried about how Katherine would react upon hearing the news Price told colleagues throughout the afternoon that if he did not come to work the next day it would be because Knight had killed him.

Everyone to whom Price mentioned this to had begged him not to go home, but he replied that if he didn't she would kill his children.

After work that evening Price arrived home to find out that Knight, although not there herself, had sent the children away for a sleep-over at a friend's house. He spent the evening with his neighbours before returning home and going to bed at around 11pm.

Katherine Knight had spent the day purchasing a new black lingerie set, visited all her children videotaping them while making comments which have since been interpreted as a crude will.

Later she returned to Price's house while he was sleeping and sat watching television for a few minutes before having a shower and changing into her new black lingerie, waking Price for sex which afterwards he fell back asleep.

A neighbour became concerned the following morning when at 6am Price's car was still in the driveway, and when Price didn't arrive for his shift at work his employer sent a worker to his residence to see what was wrong.

Both the neighbour and worker tried knocking on both the front door and Price's bedroom window to wake him but after noticing blood on the front door they alerted police who arrived shortly after 8am.

After failing to raise Price the officers broke down the back door to the property and found the body of John Price.

Katherine Knight was in a comatose state on his bed after taking a big mixture of pills.

She had stabbed Price with a butcher's knife while he was sleeping. According to the blood evidence Price had woken during the attack and tried to turn the light on before attempting to escape.

Evidence suggested that Knight chased him throughout the house, Price had managed to open the front door and get outside but either stumbled back inside or was dragged back into the hallway where he finally died after bleeding out.

During the night, after the attack, Knight went into Aberdeen and withdrew $1000 from Price's ATM account.

The autopsy of John Price revealed he had been stabbed at least 37 times, in both the front and back of his body, with many of the wounds extending into vital organs.

In the hours that followed his death Knight skinned Price, she had hung his skin from a meat hook on the architrave of a door to the lounge room – which police originally believed to be a curtain to the room they had pushed aside when they were earlier searching the property.

Katherine Knight then decapitated Price and cooked parts of his body, serving up the meat with baked potato, pumpkin, zucchini, cabbage, yellow squash and gravy in two settings at the dinner table, along with notes beside each plate, each containing the name of one of Price's children on it – she was preparing to serve his body parts to his children.

A third meal was thrown on the back lawn for unknown reasons, it was speculated by investigators that Knight had attempted to eat it but couldn't.

During her court appearance the claim was put to her, however her defence team stated that due to the intake of the pills she had consumed to take her own life that Knight had no recollection of the crime.

Price's head was found in a pot with the vegetables, the pot was still warm estimated to be at between 40 and 50 degrees

Celsius, indicating that the cooking had taken place in the early morning.

Sometime later Knight arranged the body with the left arm draped over an empty 1.25 litre soft drink bottle with the legs crossed.

This was claimed in court to be an act of defilement demonstrating Knight's contempt for Price. Knight had left a handwritten note on top of a photograph of Price. Blood stained and covered with small pieces of flesh the note read:

Time got you back Johathon for rapping [raping] my douter [daughter]. *You to Beck* [Price's daughter] *for Ross – for Little John* [his son]. *Now play with little Johns Dick John Price. (sic)*

The accusations in the note were found to be groundless.

At trial Knight's initial offer to plead guilty to manslaughter was rejected and she was arraigned on the 2nd February 2001 on the charge of murdering Price, to which she entered a plea of not guilty.

Her trial was initially fixed for the 23rd July 2001 but was adjourned to her counsel's illness and was re-fixed for the 15th October 2001.

When the trial finally commenced, Justice Barry O'Keefe offered the 60 jury prospects the option of being excused due to the nature of the photographic evidence, of which five accepted.

When the witness list was read out to the prospects several more also dropped out after which the jury was empanelled.

Knight's attorneys then spoke to the judge who adjourned to the following day; the next morning, Katherine Knight changed her plea to guilty, and the jury was dismissed.

On the 8th of November 2001, Justice O'Keefe pointed out that the nature of the crime and Knight's lack of remorse required a severe penalty.

He sentenced her to life imprisonment, refused to fix a non-parole period and ordered that her papers be marked "never to be released", the first time that this had been imposed on a woman in Australian history.

In June 2006, Katherine Knight appealed the life sentence, claiming that a penalty of life in jail without the possibility of parole was too severe for the killing.

Justices Peter McClellan, Michael Adams and Megan Latham dismissed the appeal in the NSW Court of Criminal Appeal in September of that year with Justice McClellan writing in his judgement "This was an appalling crime, almost beyond contemplation in a civilized society."

IVAN MILAT
THE BACKPACKER MUDERER

For many young adults around the world the idea to backpack across Australia, working their way from destination to destination is more than a dream – for many it is an enlightening pilgrimage.

With the ever-loveable larrikin, Mr. Crocodile Dundee Paul Hogan himself inviting them through his Tourism Australia advertisement to have a shrimp that he has thrown on the 'barbie' for them it became the land of opportunity, possibility, and adventure.

But the desire to explore Australia came to a halt when between 1989 and 1993 the bodies of seven missing young people aged between 19 and 22 were discovered partially buried in the Belanglo State Forest, 15 kilometres (9.3mi) south-west of the New South Wales town of Berrima.

Five of the victims were foreign backpackers visiting Australia (three German, two British), and two were Australian travellers from Melbourne.

It was Saturday the 19th September 1992, when two runners orienteering in the Belanglo State Forest in New South Wales, discovered a decaying corpse.

The following day, police constables Roger Gough and Suzanne Roberts discovered a second body 30 metres (98 ft) from the first.

Early media reports regarding the discovery of the bodies suggested that the bodies were that of missing British backpackers Caroline Clarke and Joanne Walters, who had disappeared from the inner Sydney suburb of Kings Cross in April 1992.

However, a German couple, Gabor Neugebauer and Anja Habschied, had also disappeared from the Kings Cross area sometime after the 25th of December 1991, and Simone Schmidl, also from Germany, had been reported missing for more than a year.

It was also possible that the bodies were a young Victorian couple, Deborah Everist and James Gibson, who had been missing since leaving the Melbourne suburb of Frankston in 1989.

Police quickly confirmed, however, that the bodies that had been discovered were those of Caroline Clarke and Joanne Walters.

Walters had been stabbed 14 times, including four times in the chest, once in the neck and nine times in the back. According to medical report the stab wounds to her spine would have paralysed her.

The zip of her jeans had been undone, but the top button was still fastened, as if she had been partially stripped and sexually assaulted, then button up hastily after the attack.

Her remains were too badly decomposed for medical investigators to establish whether a sexual attack had taken place.

Caroline Clarke had been shot ten times in the head, NSW Police investigators believing she had been used as target practice. There were groups of wounds on the back of her head and on either side of her skull.

A primitive brick fireplace had been constructed near the bodies, a cigarette butt, and spent .22-caliber cartridge cases were also recovered from the scene.

Despite an extensive search of the surrounding are over the following five days, no further evidence or bodies were found by police. Investigators made the brave decision to announce to the media that they have ruled out the possibility of further discoveries within Belanglo State Forest.

In October 1993, a local man, Bruce Pryor, discovered a human skull and femur in a particularly remote section of the forest. Panicked he raced to the local police station and return to the position where he had found the bones earlier.

With police on the scene two more bodies were quickly discovered and identified as those of Deborah Everist and James Gibson.

Thee duo had last been seen in 1989, Despite the environmental damage wrought on the clothing, Gibson's zipper was intact, it was open, but with the top button fastened, in a similar manner to Joanne Walters,

Gibson's skeleton showed eight stab wounds, a large knife had cut through his upper spine causing paralysis. Stab wounds to his back and chest would have punctured his heart and lungs.

Deborah Everist had been savagely beaten, her skull fractured in two places, her jaw was broken and there were knife marks on her forehead. She had been stabbed once in the back.

Under Post-mortem examination it was revealed that the strike to the backs of the latest victims were inflicted in a similar manner to the earlier British victims, which would result is the paralysing of the victims.

The presence of Gibson's body in Belanglo was a puzzle to investigators as his backpack and camera had previously been discovered on the side of the road at Galson Gorge, in the northern Sydney suburbs over 120 kilometres (75 mi) to the north.

On the 1st of November 1993, a skull was found in a clearing in the forest by police sergeant Jeff Trichter. The skull was later identified as that of Simone Schmidl from Regensburg, Germany.

She was last seen hitchhiking on the 20th of January 1991. Clothing at the scene however were not those of Schmidl's, but matched the description of another missing backpacker, Anja Habschied.

Schmidl's skeleton showed eight stab wounds; there may have been more. Two had severed her spine, others had punctured her heart and lungs.

The bodies of Habschied and her boyfriend Gabor Neugebauer were found on the 3rd of November 1993 in shallow graves 50 metres (160ft) apart, Habschied had been decapitated, but, despite an extensive search, her head has never been found. Neugebauer had been shot in the head six times. Three bullets entered at the base of the head and three more from the left-hand side.

New South Wales Police were now convinced that they had a serial killer on their hands, something unheard off in Australia, and started a task force to track down the murderer.

There were similar aspects to all the murders. Each of the bodies had been deliberately posed face-down with their hands behind their backs, covered by pyramidal frame of sticks and ferns.

Forensic study determined that each had suffered multiple stab wounds to the torso. The killer had evidently spent considerable time with the victims both during and after the murders, as campsites were discovered close to the location of each body and shell casings of the same calibre were also identified at each site.

Walters and Schmidl had been stabbed, whereas Clarke and Neugebauer had been shot numerous times in the head and stabbed post-mortem.

Habschied had been decapitated and other victims showed signs of strangulation and severe beatings. New South Wales Police speculated that the crimes were the work of several killers, at least two.

After developing a profile of the killer, the police faced an enormous volume of data from numerous sources. Investigators therefore applied link analysis technology to the Roads and Traffic Authority vehicle records, gym memberships, gun licensing, and internal police records. As a result, the list of suspected was progressively narrowed from an extensive list of individuals to a short list of 230, and then an even shorter list of 32.

On the 13th of November 1993, New South Wales police received a call from Paul Onions in the United Kingdom. Onions had been backpacking in Australia several years before and, while out hiking, he had accepted a ride south out of Sydney from a man only known as "Bill" on the 25th of January 1990.

South of the town of Mittagong, just 30 kilometres from the Belanglo State Forest, "Bill" pulled out some ropes and attempted to tie Onions by the hands and then pulled a gun on him, at which point he managed to escape the vehicle.

While running away from "Bill", Paul Onions, heard two shots being fired before Onions was able to flag down Joanne Berry, a passing motorist, and reported the assault to local police.

Onions' statement was backed up by Berry, who also contacted the investigation team, along with the girlfriend of a man who worked with Ivan Milat, who thought he should be questioned over the case.

On the 13th of April 1994, Detective Gordon found the note regarding Onions' call to the hotline five months earlier. Superintendent Clive Small immediately called for the original report from Bowral police – where the statements were made – but it was missing from their files.

Fortunately, Constable Janet Nicolson had taken a full report in her notebook, which provided more details than the original statement.

While looking at phone records, and work attendance records for their suspect investigators were able to confirm that Richard Milat, brother to Ivan, had been working on the day of the attack, but Ivan had not.

Ivan Robert Marko Milat was born on 27th December 1944 in Guildford, New South Wales, Australia. He is the son of Croatian emigrant Stijphan Marko Milat (1902 – 23 April 1983) and his Australian wife Margaret Elizabeth Milat (13 September 1920 – 6 October 2001).

Ivan was the fifth-born in a family that consisted of fourteen children. At the time of his arrest for the Backpacker Murders he was employed by the NSW Roads and Transport.

Family life was rural and insular, and the Milat's' predominantly kept to themselves, making reliable information about the upbringing of Ivan Milat extremely difficult to obtain.

After Milat's conviction for the 'Backpacker Murders', as they were called on news bulletins around the world, Milat's brother Boris conducted interviews where in one he indicated that Ivan had exhibited psychopathic tendencies early on, although other family members dispute this.

Ivan Milat was described as a good-looking, muscular boy, who had a fascination for hunting and guns. It is also said that he took great care of his appearance.

His parents were hard working and strict, with 14 children to manage, discipline was difficult, and Milat and his brothers had a reputation for lawlessness in their neighbourhood.

The family ensured numerous police visits to their fame as the children grew older.

From the age of 17 Milat was constantly in trouble with both the police and the courts, on charges as varied as housebreaking, car thefts and armed robberies.

In 1971, Milat was put on trial for the alleged rape of two female hitchhikers, who testified that he had been armed with a knife during the attacks. He was acquitted on the rape charges when the prosecution failed to make a convincing case against him.

When New South Wales Police Investigators continued to hear the name Ivan Milat throughout their investigation process, and saw he was one of the 32-names they had earlier narrowed down to, they began extensive investigations on the suspect.

They soon learned that both Ivan Milat and his brother Richard worked together on the road-gang working on the highways between Sydney and Melbourne.

Milat owned a property near the Belanglo, and shortly after the bodies of Caroline Clarke and Joanne Walters were discovered he sold a Nissan-Patrol four-wheeled drive vehicle.

After receiving a phone call from Paul Onions investigators then reviewed the report relating to the attempted abduction of Onions, where they noticed a harrowing similarity between the abduction attempt and the murders that had been committed.

At the request of New South Wales Police Paul Onions flew from his home in the United Kingdom to Sydney, Australia, to further assist them with their investigation.

On the 5th of May 1994, Onions positively identified Ivan Milat from a photo line up as the man who had picked him up and attempted to tie him up.

Fifty heavily armed police officers surrounded a house in the quiet suburb of Eagle Vale on the 22nd of May, where they executed an arrest and search warrant on Ivan Milat.

The homes of his brothers Richard, Alex, Boris, Walter and Bill were also searched at the same time by 300 other police officers.

Inside the home in Cinnabar Street, where the residents from neighbouring properties had their peace broken by the commotion going on Police found a cache of weapons, including parts of a .22-calibre riffle that matched the type used in the murders.

Clothing, camping equipment, and cameras belonging to several of the victims were also found in various hidden locations throughout the property, all were taken as evidence.

Milat appeared in court on robbery and weapon charges on the 23rd of May. He did not enter a plea during his court appearance. Following further investigations, Milat was also charged with the murders of seven backpackers.

In March 1996 the trial of Ivan Milat began, and lasted fifteen weeks. Milat's defence argued that, despite the evidence, there was no proof that Ivan Milat was guilty and attempted to shift the blame onto other family members, in particular his brother Richard.

On 27th July 1996, a jury found Ivan Milat guilty of the murders. He was also convicted of the attempted murder, false imprisonment and robbery of Paul Onions – for which he received six years imprisonment each.

For the murders of Caroline Clarke, Joanne Walters, Simone Schmidl, Anja Habschied, Gabor Neugebauer, James Gibson and Deborah Everist, Ivan Milat was given a life sentence on each count, running consecutively and without the possibility of parole.

Police maintain that Ivan Milat may have been involved in many more murders than the seven he was convicted for. In 2001 Milat was ordered to give evidence at an inquest into the disappearances of three other female backpackers.

Similar inquiries launched in 2003, in relation to the disappearance of two nurses and again in 2005, in relation to the disappearance of hitchhiker Anette Briffa – no additional charges against Ivan Milat have been laid as a result of these inquiries with police stating a lack of evidence as the main reason.

MARTIN BRYANT
THE PORT ARTHUR MASSACRE

Australians were shocked, outraged and shaken to their core when, on the evening of Sunday 28th April 1996, they learned that over 30 people had been murdered and countless others injured at the Port Arthur Historical Site (PAHS) in Tasmania. One of the countries most venerable historical sites, and adjacent locations.

Port Arthur is a small town and former convict settlement on the Tasman Peninsula and is one of Australia's most significant heritage areas.

The site forms part of the Australian Convict Sites, a World Heritage property consisting of eleven remnant penal sites originally built within the British Empire during the 18th and 19th centuries on fertile Australian costal strips.

Collectively these sites, including Port Arthur, now represent, "… the best surviving examples of large scale convict transportation and the colonial expansion of European powers through the presence and labour of convicts."

The Port Arthur Historical Site is located approximately 97 kilometres (60 miles) south-east of the state capital of Hobart.

Martin John Bryant was born on the 7th of May 1967 in the Tasmanian capital Hobart. He was the first son born to Maurice and Carleen Bryant.

Although the family home was in Lenah Valley, Bryant spent a large part of his childhood growing up at their beach house in Carnarvon Bay.

Bryant was described as being distant from reality and unemotional by teachers. While his mother in a 2011 interview said that Martin Bryant was an *"annoying"* and *"different"* child.

At school he was a disruptive and sometimes violent student, who suffered severe bullying by other children. After getting suspended from New Town Primary School in 1977, psychological assessments of Bryant indicated that he enjoyed torturing animals.

He returned to school the following year with improved behaviour, however, he persisted in teaching younger children. Martin Bryant was transferred to a special education unit at New Town High School in 1980 where he deteriorated both academically and in behaviour throughout his remaining school years.

Descriptions of Martin Bryant as an adolescent show that he continued to be disturbed and outlined the possibility of an intellectual disability.

He was revealed to be borderline mentally disabled with an I.Q of 66, equivalent to that of an 11-year-old child in the tenth percentile – 90% of 11-year-olds would score higher.

On leaving school Bryant was accessed for a disability pension by a psychiatrist who wrote *"Cannot read or write. Does a bit of gardening and watches T.V… only his parents' efforts prevent further deterioration. Could be schizophrenic and parents face a bleak future with him."*

While awaiting trial, for the Port Arthur Massacre, Martin Bryant was examined by a court-appointed psychiatrist Ian Sale, who believed Bryant *"could be regarded as having shown a mixture of conduct disorder, attention deficit hyperactivity, and a rare condition known as Autism."*

In early 1987 a then 19-year-old Martin Bryant met the 54-year-old Helen Mary Elizabeth Harvey, heiress to a share in the Tattersall's Lottery fortune, while looking for new clients for his lawn mowing business.

Harvey, who was living with her mother Hilza, befriended Bryant who became a regular visitor to her neglected mansion and assisted with tasks such as feeding the fourteen dogs living inside the house, and the forty cats that lived in her garage.

In June 1990 someone reported Harvey to the health authorities, and medics found both Harvey and her mother Hilza in urgent need of hospital treatment. A few weeks later the 79-year-old Hilza Harvey died.

A clean-up order was placed on the mansion and Bryant's father Maurice took long service leave from his job to help clean the interior of the property.

Soon after Harvey invited Martin Bryant to move in with her, and they began spending large amounts of money, which included, the purchase of thirty new cars in the space of three years.

The couple began to spend most days shopping, often having lunch at a local restaurant. Around this time Martin was reassessed for his disability pension with a note on his file reading:

"Father protects him from any occasion that may upset him as he continuously threatens violence… Martin tells me he would like to go around shooting people. It would be unsafe to allow Martin out of his parents control."

In 1991, because of no longer being allowed animals at the house, Harvey and Bryant moved together to a 29-hectare (72 acre) farm called Taurusville.

Neighbours recall that Bryant always carried an airgun which he often fired at tourists as they stopped by to buy apples from a stall on the other side of the highway.

Bryant reportedly under the cover of darkness would roam through the surrounding properties and would shoot at dogs who would bark at him. Everyone tried their best to avoid him despite his attempts to befriend them.

On October 20th, 1992 Helen Harvey was killed when her car veered on to the wrong side of the road and hit an oncoming vehicle going in the opposite direction.

Bryant was inside the vehicle at the time of the accident and was hospitalised for seven months with severe neck and back injuries. He was briefly investigated by police for the role he played in the accident, as Bryant had a known habit of lunging for the steering wheel and Harvey had already had three accidents because of Bryant doing this.

Bryant was named the sole beneficiary in Harvey's will and came into assets totalling more than $550 000. As Bryant only had the vaguest notion of financial matters, his mother applied for and was granted a guardianship order, placing Bryant's assets under the management of Public Trustees. The order was based on evidence of Bryant's diminished intellectual capacity.

After Harvey's death, Bryant's father Maurice looked after the Copping farm. Bryant returned to the family home to convalesce after leaving hospital.

Two months later, on 14th August 1993, a visitor looking for Maurice Bryant at the Copping Farm found a note saying "call the police" pinned to the front door and found several thousand dollars in his car.

The rates officer at the time found no reason to suspect criminal intent and sent council members and police to quell the stresses put forward by letters sent to the Local Council Chambers.

Police searched the property for Maurice Bryant, without success. Divers were called in to search the four dams on the property and on the 16th of August, his body was found in the dam closest to the farmhouse with one of Martin Bryant's diving weight belts around his neck.

Police described the death as "unnatural" and it was ruled a suicide. Martin inherited the proceeds of his superannuation fund, valued at $250 000.

Family members state that it was unusual to her the alarm go off at 6 a.m., none had ever known him to use it before as he has no work and no other commitments.

At 8 a.m. his girlfriend left the house that he had inherited from Helen Harvey, to go and visit her parents, after getting ready for what he had planned for the day Bryant left the house at 9.47 a.m. at which time he engaged the alarm, which registered the time.

It was approximately 10:30a.m. when the yellow Volvo driven by Martin Bryant pulled into the small carpark at the Midway Point Newsagency, after checking that they sold cigarette lighters Bryant purchased one using a large note and not waiting around for his change.

Paying with coins Bryant then purchased a bottle of tomato sauce from the Sorell Supermarket before continuing his trip arriving at Forcett Village shortly after 11a.m. where he purchased a cup of coffee from the Shell Service Station.

Making small talk with the attendant behind the counter Martin Bryant claimed he was heading out to go surfing at Roaring Beach, the attendant noted that it was a very calm day.

Bryant then drove past Eaglehawk Neck area and stopped at the service station "Convict Bakery" to purchase $15 worth of petrol.

The attendant saw Bryant staring at the bay and its calm water. Bryant had a surf board on the roof rack of his yellow Volvo and the attendant also noted that the surfing conditions that day were poor.

He continued down to Port Arthur and was seen driving into Seascape down the Arthur Highway around 11:45. He stopped at the Seascape guest accommodation site that his father had wanted to purchase, owned by David and Sally Martin.

Bryant went inside and fired several shots, then gagged David Martin and stabbed him. Witnesses testified to different numbers of shots fired at this time. It was claimed in court that it was believed that this was the time that Bryant killed the Martins.

A couple stopped at Seascape and Bryant appeared outside. They asked if they could have a look at the accommodation. Bryant told them that they could not because his parents were away and his girlfriend was inside.

His demeanour was described as quite rude and the couple felt uncomfortable. They left at about 12:35 p.m. Bryant's car was seen reversed up to the front door where it is believed that he unloaded a stockpile of ammunition.

Bryant drove to Port Arthur, taking the keys to the Seascape properties after locking the doors. Bryant stopped at a car which had pulled over from overheating and talked with two people there. He suggested that they come to the Port Arthur cafe for some coffee later.

He travelled past the Port Arthur historic site toward a Palmer's Lookout Road property owned by the Martins, where he came across Roger Larner driving out of his driveway.

Larner had met him on some occasions over 15 years ago but did not initially recognise him. Bryant told Larner he had been surfing and had bought a property called Fogg Lodge and was now looking to buy some cattle from Larner.

Bryant also made several comments about buying the Martins' place next door. He asked if Marian Larner was home, and asked if he could continue down the driveway of the farm to see her.

Larner said it was okay however told Bryant he would come also. Bryant changed his mind and left, claiming he was going to return in the afternoon.

At around 1:10 p.m., Bryant got in line behind other cars at the toll booth at the entrance to the historic site. Upon getting close to the toll booth, he left the line and moved to the back again.

Eventually getting to the front of the line, he claimed someone almost reversed into him. He paid the entry fee and proceeded to park near the Broad Arrow Cafe, near the water's edge.

The site security manager told him to park with the other cars because that area was reserved for camper-vans and the car park was very busy that day.

Bryant moved his car to another area and sat in his car for a few minutes. He then moved his car back near the water, outside the cafe.

The security manager saw him go up to the cafe carrying a large bag and a video camera, but didn't really take much notice of him.

Bryant went into the cafe and purchased a meal, which he ate on the deck outside. People held the door open for him and commented on the large amount of food he had. He replied that he was hungry from surfing.

Bryant started conversations with several people about **European wasps in the area and the lack of Japanese** tourists, but seemed to be mainly mumbling and ranting to himself.

He appeared nervous and continually looked back to the car-park and into the cafe.

Bryant finished his meal, walked into the cafe and returned his tray, assisted by some people who opened the door for him.

He put down his bag on a table and pulled out an AR-15 rifle with one 30-round magazine attached. He left the bag which contained, among other things, the knife with which he had stabbed Martin, on the table.

It is believed the magazine was partially emptied from the previous rounds fired at Seascape.

The cafe was very small with the tables very close together. The cafe was particularly busy that day as people waited for the next ferry. The series of events happened extremely quickly.

Bryant took aim from his hip and pointed his rifle at Moh Yee (William) Ng and Sou Leng Chung, who were visiting from Malaysia, who were at a table beside Bryant.

He shot them at close range, killing both instantly. Bryant lifted the rifle to his shoulder and fired a shot at Mick Sargent, grazing his scalp and knocking him to the floor.

He fired a fourth shot, a fatal one that hit Sargent's girlfriend, 21-year-old Kate Elizabeth Scott, in the back of the head.

A 28-year-old New Zealand winemaker, Jason Winter, had been helping the staff at the busy cafe. As Bryant turned towards Winter's wife, Joanne, and their 15-month-old son, Mitchell, Winter threw a serving tray at Bryant in an attempt to distract him. Joanne Winter's father pushed his daughter and grandson to the floor and under the table.

Anthony Nightingale stood up after the sound of the first shots, but had no time to move. Nightingale yelled "*No, not here!*" as Bryant pointed the weapon at him. As Nightingale leaned forward, he was fatally shot through the neck and spine.

The next table had held a group of ten friends, but some had just left the table to return their meal trays and visit the gift shop.

Bryant fired one shot that hit Kevin Vincent Sharp, 68, killing him. The second hit Walter Bennett, passed through his body and struck Raymond John Sharp, 67, Kevin Sharp's brother, killing both.

The three had their backs towards Bryant, and were unaware what was happening. One of them even made the comment *"That's not funny"* after hearing the first few shots, not realising it was a real gun.

The shots were all close range, with the gun at, or just inches away from, the back of their heads. Gerald Broome, Gaye Fidler and her husband John were all struck by bullet fragments, but survived.

Bryant then turned towards Tony and Sarah Kistan and Andrew Mills. Both men stood up at the noise of the initial shots but had no time to move away. Andrew Mills was shot in the head. Tony Kistan was also shot from about two metres away, also in the head, but had managed to push his wife away prior to being shot. Sarah Mills was apparently not seen by Bryant, as she was under the table by that time.

Thelma Walker and Pamelia Law were injured by shrapnel before being dragged to the ground by their friend, Peter Crosswell, as the three sheltered underneath the table. Also injured by fragments from these shots was Patricia Barker.

It was only then that the majority of the people in the cafe began to realise what was happening and that the shots were not some sort of noise from a re-enactment at the historical site.

At this point there was great confusion, with many people not knowing what to do, as Bryant was near the main exit.

Bryant moved just a few metres and began shooting at another table, where Graham Colyer, Carolyn Loughton and her daughter Sarah were seated.

Colyer was injured in the jaw, causing him to nearly choke to death on his own blood. Sarah Loughton ran towards her mother who had been moving between tables.

Carolyn Loughton threw herself on top of her daughter. Bryant shot Carolyn Loughton in the back, her eardrum ruptured by the **sonic boom** from the gun going off beside her ear.

Carolyn Loughton survived her injuries, although her daughter was shot in the head. The elder Loughton did not discover until she came out of surgery that despite her efforts, Sarah was fatally injured.

Bryant pivoted around and fatally shot Mervyn Howard, a football administrator, who was still seated. The bullet travelled through him, through a window of the cafe, and hit a table on the outside balcony.

Bryant quickly followed up with a shot to the neck of Mervyn Howard's wife, Elizabeth. The gunman Martin Bryant then leaned over a vacant baby stroller and pointed the gun at her head and shot her a second time.

Both of the Howards' injuries were fatal. Several people outside then realised there was real danger and began to run away.

Bryant was near the exit, preventing others from attempting to run past him and escape. Bryant moved across the cafe towards the gift shop area.

There was an exit door through the display area to the outside balcony, but it was locked and could only be opened with a key. As Bryant moved along, Robert Elliott stood up, perhaps hoping to distract Bryant. He was shot in the arm and head, left slumping against the fireplace but alive.

All of these events, from the first bullet that killed Ng, took approximately 15 seconds, during which 12 people were dead and 10 more were wounded.

Bryant moved toward the gift shop area, giving many people time to hide under tables and behind shop displays. He shot the two local women who worked in the gift shop, Nicole Burgess, 17, and Elizabeth Howard, 26. Burgess was shot in the head and Howard in the arm and chest. Both succumbed to their injuries.

Coralee Lever and Vera Jary hid behind a hessian screen with others. Lever's husband, Dennis, was shot in the head and died.

Pauline Masters, Vera Jary's husband Ron, and Peter and Carolyn Nash had attempted to escape through a locked door but could not.

Peter Nash lay down on top of his wife to hide her from Bryant. Bryant moved into the gift shop area where people, trapped with nowhere to go, were crouched down in the corners.

Gwen Neander, trying to escape through the door, was shot in the head and killed.

Bryant saw movement in the café and moved near the front door. He shot at a table and hit Peter Crosswell, who was hiding under it, in the buttock.

Jason Winter, hiding in the gift shop, thought Bryant had left the building and made some comment about it to people near him before moving out into the open.

Bryant saw him, with Winter stating *"No, no"* just prior to being shot, the bullet hitting his hand, neck and chest. A second shot to the head proved fatal to Winter.

Fragments from those shots struck American tourist Dennis Olson who had been hiding with his wife, Mary, and Winter Dennis Olson suffered shrapnel injuries to his hand, scalp, eye and chest, but survived the injuries.

It is not clear what happened next, although at some point, Bryant reloaded his weapon. Bryant walked back to the cafe and then returned to the gift shop, this time looking down to another corner of the shop where he found several people hiding in the corner, trapped.

He walked up to them and shot Ronald Jary through the neck, killing him. He then shot Peter Nash and Pauline Masters, killing both of them. He did not see Carolyn Nash who was lying under her husband.

Bryant aimed his gun at an unidentified Asian man, but the rifle's magazine was empty. Bryant then quickly moved to the gift shop counter where he reloaded his rifle, leaving an empty magazine on the service counter and left the building.

29 rounds were fired in the cafe and gift shop areas in approximately 90–120 seconds. In that time, Bryant had killed 20 people.

During the cafe shooting, some staff members had been able to escape through the kitchen and alert people outside. There were a number of coaches outside with lines of people, many of whom began to hide in the buses or in nearby buildings.

Others did not understand the situation or were not sure where to go. Some people believed there was some sort of historical re-enactment happening, and moved towards the area.

Ashley John Law, a site employee, was moving people away from the café into the information centre when Bryant fired at him from 50–100 metres away. The bullets missed Law and hit some trees nearby.

Bryant then moved down towards the coaches. One of the coach drivers, Royce Thompson, was shot in the back as he was moving along the passengers' side of a coach.

He fell to the ground and was able to crawl, then roll under the bus to safety, but he later died of his wounds. Brigid Cook was trying to guide a number of people down between the buses and along the jetty area to cover.

She had only been informed of what was happening and was worried that she was making a fool of herself in over-reacting, although her actions no doubt saved many lives.

Bryant then moved to the front of this bus and walked across to the next coach. People had quickly moved from this coach towards the back end, in an attempt to seek cover. As Bryant walked around it he saw people scrambling to hide and shot at them. Brigid Cook was shot in the right thigh, causing the bone to fragment, the bullet lodging there.

A coach driver, Ian McElwee, was hit by fragments of Miss Cook's bone. Both were able to escape and survived.

Bryant then quickly moved around another coach and fired at another group of people. Winifred Aplin, running to get to cover behind another coach, was fatally shot in the side. Another bullet grazed Yvonne Lockley's cheek, but she was able to enter one of the coaches to hide, and survived

Some people then started moving away from the car park towards the jetty. But someone shouted that Bryant was moving that way, so they tried to double back around the coaches to where Brigid Cook was previously shot.

Bryant doubled back to where Janet and Neville Quin, who owned a wildlife park on the east coast of Tasmania, were beginning to move toward Mason Cove and away from the buses.

Bryant shot Janet Quin in the back, where she fell, unable to move, near Royce Thompson.

Bryant then continued along the car park as people tried to escape along the shore. Doug Hutchinson was attempting to get into a coach when he was shot in the arm.

He quickly changed directions, ran around the front of the coach, and then along the shore to the jetty and hid.

Bryant then went to his vehicle, which was just past the coaches, and changed weapons to the **FN FAL**. He fired at Denise Cromer, who was near the penitentiary ruins.

Gravel flew up in front of her, as the bullets hit the ground. Bryant then got in his car and sat there for a few moments before getting out again and moving back to the coaches.

Some people were taking cover behind cars in the car park, and because of the elevation, Bryant could see them and the cars did not provide much cover.

When they realised Bryant had seen them, they ran into the bush. He fired several shots, at least one hit a tree behind which someone was taking cover, but no-one was hit.

Bryant moved back to the buses where Janet Quin laid injured from the earlier shot. Bryant shot her in the back, then left; she later died from her wounds.

Bryant then went onto one of the coaches and fired a shot at Elva Gaylard who was on the bus hiding, hitting her in the arm and chest, killing her.

At an adjacent coach, Gordon Francis saw what happened and moved down the aisle to try and shut the door of the coach he was on. He was seen by Bryant and shot from the opposite coach. He survived but needed four major operations.

Neville Quin, husband of Janette, had escaped to the jetty area, but had come back to look for his wife. He had been forced to leave her earlier after Bryant had shot her.

Bryant exited the coach and noticing Quin, chased Quin around the coaches as he tried to escape. Bryant fired at him at least twice before Quin ran onto a coach, in the hope of escaping Bryant.

Bryant entered the coach and pointed the gun at Neville Quin's face, saying, "*No one gets away from me*". Mr Quin ducked when he realised Bryant was about to pull the trigger. The bullet missed his head but hit his neck, momentarily paralysing him.

After Bryant had left, Quin managed to find his wife, although she later died in his arms. Neville Quin was eventually taken away by helicopter and survived.

As Bryant left the coach, James Balasko, an American citizen, tried to catch Bryant on his video camera. He was successful but Bryant saw him and fired at him, hitting a nearby car.

By now many people, unable to use their parked cars, were hiding or running along Jetty Road or the jetty itself. Most people did not know where Bryant was because the gunfire was extremely loud and difficult to pinpoint.

It was not clear that Bryant was mobile, nor was it even clear from which direction the shots were coming.

Bryant then got back into his car and proceeded to leave the car park. Witnesses say he was sounding the horn and waving, others say he was also firing.

Bryant drove along Jetty Road towards the toll booth where a number of people were running away. Bryant passed by at least two people. Ahead of him were Nanette Mikac (Née Moulton) and her two young children, Madeline, 3, and Alannah, 6 years old.

Nanette was carrying Madeline and Alannah was running slightly ahead. By now they had run approximately 600 metres from the car park. Nanette told Alannah, *"We're safe now, pumpkin."*

Bryant opened his door and slowed down. Mikac moved towards the car, apparently thinking he was offering them help in escaping.

Several more people witnessed this from further down the road. Someone then recognised him as the gunman and yelled out *"It's him!"*.

Bryant stepped out of the car, put his hand on Nanette Mikac's shoulder and told her to get on her knees. She did so, saying, *"Please don't hurt my babies"*

Bryant shot her in the temple, killing her, before firing a shot at Madeleine, which hit her in the shoulder, before shooting her fatally through the chest.

Bryant shot twice at Alannah, as she ran behind the tree, missing. He then walked up, pressed the barrel of the gun into her neck and fired, killing her instantly.

Martin Bryant fired one or two more rounds at some people hiding in a bush, but he missed. Having seen the murders of the children, some people further up the road began running.

They told drivers of cars coming down the road to go back. The good Samaritans thought Bryant would head up the road, so instead they proceeded on foot down a dirt side road and hid in the bush.

The cars reversed up the road to the toll booth, and drivers stopped to ask the staff member what was happening. It appeared no one at the toll booth area knew what was happening.

Bryant drove up to the toll booth where there were several vehicles and blocked a BMW. The car was owned by Mary Rose Nixon.

The car, driven by Russell James Pollard, was also occupied by Helene and Robert Graham Salzmann. An argument with Robert Salzmann ensued, and Bryant took out the FAL and shot Salzmann at point blank range, killing him.

Pollard emerged from the BMW and went towards Bryant, who shot him in the chest, killing him. More cars then arrived, seeing this, but were quickly able to reverse back up the road. Bryant then moved to the BMW and pulled Nixon and Helene Salzmann from the car and shot them dead, dragging their bodies onto the road.

Bryant transferred ammunition, handcuffs, the AR-15 rifle and a fuel container to the BMW. Mary Nixon, Russell Pollard, and Helene Salzmann, as well as Graham Salzmann, are the people Bryant was charged with killing at the toll booth.

Another car then came towards the toll booth and Bryant shot at it. The driver, Graham Sutherland, was hit with glass. A second bullet hit the driver's door. The car quickly reversed back up the road and left. Bryant then got into the BMW having left behind a number of items in his Volvo, including a shotgun and hundreds of rounds of ammunition.

Graham Sutherland, who just had been shot at in his car, reversed back up the road and drove to the service station close by, where he tried to inform people what was happening.

Bryant drove up to the service station and cut off a white Toyota Corolla that was attempting to exit onto the highway. Glenn Pears was driving the car with girlfriend Zoe Hall in the passenger seat.

Bryant quickly exited the car with his rifle in hand and tried to pull Hall from the car. Pears got out of the car and approached Bryant. Bryant pointed the gun at Pears and pushed him backwards, eventually directing him into the now open boot of the BMW, locking Pears inside.

Bryant then moved back to the passenger side of the Corolla as Hall attempted to climb over to the driver's seat. The gunman raised his rifle and fired three shots, killing her.

Many people around the service station saw this and ran to hide in nearby bushland. The service station attendant told everyone to lie down and he locked the main doors. He grabbed his rifle, but by the time he could retrieve some ammunition and load his gun, Bryant was back in his car and gone. A police officer arrived several minutes later and then went in the direction of Bryant.

As Bryant drove down to Seascape he shot at a red Falcon coming the other way, smashing its front windscreen. Upon arriving at Seascape, he got out of his car. A **Frontera** 4WD vehicle then approached Seascape along the road.

They saw Bryant with his gun but believed him to be rabbit hunting and actually slowed down as they passed him. Bryant fired into the car, the first bullet hit the bonnet and broke the throttle cable.

He fired at least two more bullets into the car as it passed, breaking the windows. One bullet hit the driver, Linda White, in the arm. The car was going downhill so it was able to roll down the road out of sight around a corner.

White swapped seats with her boyfriend, Michael Wanders, who attempted to drive the car but was unable to, because of the broken throttle cable.

Another vehicle then drove down the road, carrying four people. It was not until they were almost adjacent to Bryant that they realised he was carrying a gun. Bryant shot at the car, smashing the windscreen. Douglas Horner was wounded by shrapnel from the shattered windscreen.

The car proceeded ahead where White and Wanders tried to get in, but Horner did not realise the situation and drove on. When they saw that White had been shot, they came back and picked them up. Both parties then continued down to a local establishment called the Fox and Hound, where they called police.

Yet another car drove past and Bryant shot at it, hitting the passenger, Susan Williams, in the hand. The driver, Simon Williams, was struck by shrapnel.

Another approaching vehicle saw this and reversed back up the road. Bryant also fired at this car hitting it but not injuring anyone. Bryant then got back into the BMW and drove down the Seascape driveway to the house.

Sometime after he stopped, Bryant removed Pears from the boot and handcuffed him to a stair rail within the house. At some point he also set the BMW on fire with fuel. He is believed to have arrived at the house by about 2 p.m.

At 1:30 p.m. the only two police officers in the area had received a radio message to attend Port Arthur and be on the look out for a yellow Volvo.

They headed to Port Arthur in different cars, going different routes. On the way they were informed to look for the BMW and eventually they were informed of people at the Fox and Hound who had been shot.

One police officer then drove down the road past Seascape and past the disabled car of Mrs White. He looked at it for a moment and continued down to the Fox and Hound.

He informed his partner about events and they then proceeded back to Seascape. At about 2 p.m. they were back at Seascape and could see the BMW on fire.

At some point they were fired upon, and eventually had to hide in a ditch at the side of the road. Martin Bryant fired at them whenever they tried to escape, and they were not able to move from that position for many hours.

At around 2:10 p.m. Bryant received a call from a woman from the ABC network, she had been ringing local businesses randomly trying to receive information about what was occurring, and Bryant answered the Seascape phone.

Bryant informed her his name was Jamie and when she asked what was happening he replied "*Lots of fun*". Bryant then informed her that if she phoned him again, he would shoot Mr Pears.

At about 3 p.m., shortly after forcing the police officers to take cover in the ditch, Bryant rang the local police station where the girlfriend of one of the police officers answered the phone.

Bryant asked who she was and if she knew where her husband was. He also called himself Jamie. He asked if she knew or not if her husband was okay, and when she didn't answer, Bryant then told her he was okay and that he knew where her husband was.

Around 9 p.m. a team from the **Special Operations Group of the Tasmania Police h**ad arrived and were eventually able to assist in removing the policemen from the ditch to safety by using the cover of darkness, riot shields and bullet proof jackets.

They did not provide cover fire for fear of hitting hostages. An 18-hour standoff ensued during which time the police talked over the phone to Bryant who called himself 'Jamie'.

He made a request for a helicopter, saying that he wanted to be flown to a plane and then onto Adelaide in South Australia. He said that if the helicopter arrived he would release one hostage, Mr Pears, and only keep Mrs Martin.

Bryant could see the movement of SOG officers and continually demanded their retreat each time they began an approach to the house.

Police believed he had some kind of visual aid device, as he appeared to maintain excellent awareness of the events unfurling around him despite the pitch black of night, however none was ever found.

A man was spotted on the roof of an adjacent building at one point, believed to be Bryant. Later in the night, the cordless phone Bryant was using began to run low on batteries. Police tried unsuccessfully to get him to return the phone to the charger, but it went dead and no further communications were established.

Bryant was captured the following morning when he presumably started a fire in the guest house. Bryant taunted police to 'come and get him', but the police, believing the hostage was already dead, decided that the fire would eventually bring him out.

A large amount of ammunition had also ignited and was exploding sporadically as the house burned. He eventually ran out of the house with his clothes on fire and quickly removed his burning clothes. He was arrested by the police, and taken to hospital for treatment.

It was found that Mr Pears had been shot dead during or before the standoff and had died before the fire. The remains of the Martins were also found.

It was also determined they had been shot, and in the case of Mrs Martin suffered blunt force trauma. They both died before the fire and witness accounts, as presented to the Supreme Court of Tasmania, of the gunfire place the time of death of David and Sally Martin as being approximately noon on 28 April.

One weapon was found burnt in the house, and the other on the roof of the adjacent building where police believed they had seen Bryant the night before.

Both weapons had suffered from massive chamber blast pressure, possibly from the heat of the house fire. In his police interview Bryant admitted to having car jacked the BMW, but claimed it only had three occupants and denied shooting any person.

He also claimed he did not take the BMW from the vicinity of the toll booth and that his hostage was taken from the BMW. He said that he thought the man he took hostage must have died in the boot when the car exploded.

He did not distinguish between the car fire and the later house fire. He also denied visiting Port Arthur on that day, despite identification by several people including the toll attendant.

Such discrepancies indicate that Bryant was either lying during the police interview, or was mentally incapable of recalling events accurately.

Bryant also claimed that the guns found by police were not his, but admitted to owning the shotgun that was found with his passport back in his own car near the toll booth.

Initially Bryant pleaded not guilty to the 35 murders, laughing hysterically as the judge read out the charges against him. He later changed his plea to guilty after being sent back to solitary confinement.

Bryant did not provide a confession. He was found guilty of all charges and is now serving 35 sentences of life imprisonment (for the 35 murders) plus 1,035 years in Hobart's Risdon Prison (as cumulative penalty for various charges including attempted murder and grievous bodily harm for shooting at, and injuring, numerous people).

His prison papers indicate that he is never to be released. He continues to serve his term without possibility of parole. This is very rare in Australia, where the majority of murder sentences allow for the possibility of parole after a long prison term. Martin Bryant remains Australia's worst killing spree murderer and the incident is one of the worst cases worldwide of a mass killing spree in modern times.

www.ingramcontent.com/pod-product-compliance
Lightning Source LLC
Chambersburg PA
CBHW021342290326
41933CB00037B/334